Emotional
DISCIPLINE

Other Books by Charles C. Manz

The Power of Failure
Charles C. Manz

The New SuperLeadership: Leading Others to Lead Themselves
Charles C. Manz and Henry P. Sims, Jr.

The Wisdom of Solomon at Work:
Ancient Virtues for Living and Leading Today
Charles C. Manz, Karen P. Manz, Robert D. Marx, and Christopher P. Neck

Team Work and Group Dynamics
Gregory Stewart, Charles C. Manz, and Henry P. Sims, Jr.

Mastering Self-Leadership:
Empowering Yourself for Personal Excellence, Third Edition
Charles C. Manz and Christopher P. Neck

The Leadership Wisdom of Jesus:
Practical Lessons for Today
Charles C. Manz

For Team Members Only:
Making Your Workplace Team Productive and Hassle-Free
Charles C. Manz, Christopher P. Neck, James Mancuso, and Karen P. Manz

Company of Heroes: Unleashing the Power of Self-Leadership
Henry P. Sims, Jr., and Charles C. Manz

Business Without Bosses:
How Self-Managing Teams Are Building High-Performing Companies
Charles C. Manz and Henry P. Sims, Jr.

SuperLeadership: Leading Others to Lead Themselves
Charles C. Manz and Henry P. Sims, Jr.

The Art of Self-Leadership:
Strategies for Personal Effectiveness in Your Life and Work
Charles C. Manz

Emotional
DISCIPLINE
The Power to Choose How You Feel

5 Life Changing Steps to Feeling Better Every Day

CHARLES C. MANZ

BERRETT-KOEHLER PUBLISHERS, INC.
San Francisco

Berrett-Koehler Publishers, Inc.
235 Montgomery Street, Suite 650
San Francisco, CA 94104-2916
Tel: 415-288-0260   Fax: 415-362-2512
Website: www.bkconnection.com

Ordering Information

Individual sales. Berrett-Koehler publications are available through most bookstores. They can also be ordered direct from Berrett-Koehler Publishers by calling, toll-free: 800-929-2929; fax 802-864-7626.

Quantity sales. Special discounts are available on quantity purchases by corporations, associations, and others. For details, contact the "Special Sales Department" at the Berrett-Koehler address above.

Orders for college textbook/course adoption use. Please contact Berrett-Koehler Publishers toll-free: 800-929-2929; fax 802-864-7626.

Orders by U.S. trade bookstores and wholesalers. Please contact Publishers Group West, 1700 Fourth Street, Berkeley, CA 94710; 510-528-1444; 1-800-788-3123; fax 510-528-9555.

Berrett-Koehler and the BK logo are registered trademarks of Berrett-Koehler Publishers, Inc.

Printed in the United States of America

Berrett-Koehler books are printed on long-lasting acid-free paper. When it is available, we choose paper that has been manufactured by environmentally responsible processes. These may include using trees grown in sustainable forests, incorporating recycled paper, minimizing chlorine in bleaching, or recycling the energy produced at the paper mill.

Library of Congress Cataloging-in-Publication Data
Manz, Charles C.
 Emotional discipline : the power to choose how you feel / by Charles C. Manz.
   p. cm.
 Includes bibliographical references and index.
 ISBN 1-57675-230-5
 1. Emotions. 2. Emotional intelligence. I. Title.
 BF531.M27 2002
 154.2—dc21   2002033213

07 06 05 04 03   10 9 8 7 6 5 4 3 2 1

Copyeditor: Patricia Brewer; Text design: Detta Penna, Compositor/production service: Penna Design & Production; Indexer: Joan Dickey

~~~~~~~~~~~~~~

I dedicate this book
to my primary Emotional Discipline Team,
which has challenged me to be a more conscious
and emotionally complete human being
through both the great times and the difficult
(but still great) ones—
My family
Karen
Chris
and Katy.
I only hope I have done the same for them.

~~~~~~~~~~~~

Contents

~~~~~~~

Preface

~ ~ ~ ~ ~ ~ ~

Let me begin with a confession—I am emotionally challenged. I do care what people think and I would very much like it if you approved of this book. I can be sensitive and defensive at times and I struggle with criticism. I get nervous before I make a public presentation, which is a regular part of my work, and I sometimes feel afraid when I face new challenges. I enjoy approval, I need to feel accepted and loved, and I can feel angry when I believe that I've been treated unfairly. I have experienced jealousy, anxiety, irritability, longing, desire, pride, boredom, shame, laziness, worry, embarrassment, and feeling overwhelmed. I've also felt enthusiastic, calm, hopeful, vibrant, inspired, courageous, happy and even a sense of love. . . . Well, you get the idea.

I am indeed emotionally challenged, but then aren't we all? After all, emotions are what add feeling to our lives and elevate them beyond the sterile and mundane. I think of our emotions and how we feel as enriching life in a way similar to what vibrant color adds to sight, music to hearing, perfume to scent, and chocolate to taste.

And our emotional state can have a major impact on our energy level. How often do we hear a comment like "I just wish I had more energy to accomplish all that I need to do" or "I only have so much energy so I need to be selective in what activities I choose to be involved with." Yet a more helpful comment, and one that is more appropriate for this book, might be something like "I only have so much energy unless I learn to create more, so I need to make wise moment-to-moment choices that will influence how I feel and consequently help me increase my energy rather than drain it."

For example, feeling upset can be very draining. We can use up (and often waste) a great deal of energy when our emotions heat up. Anger, resentment, anxiety, fear, and many other often toxic emotions can poke large holes in our energy reservoir and drain the life out of us. Even less dramatic feelings such as boredom, indifference, apathy, and purposelessness, can slowly suck us dry. Yet other feelings, such as purposefulness, balance, personal growth, inspiration, timelessness, flow, and love can feed our energy system and actually increase it.

I have experienced all these things in my own life, and often with a good dose of struggle along the way. Gradually, however, through my personal studies, research, observations, and life experiences I have become increasingly aware of the power we have to choose how we feel. Over time, I have identified and developed strategies to help effectively create this life-enriching process. Most of my writing and speaking over the past 20 years has focused on a concept I call "self-leadership"—the overall process and various specific strategies we use to create the motivation and direction we need to cope with and even thrive in our life and work. In this book I am specifically focusing on probably the most potent part of this process—our emotions and feelings. Specifically, I call the overall process of choosing how we feel *Emotional Discipline.*

I have come to realize that the choices we make on a day-to-day, moment-to-moment basis hold the key to influencing the way we feel. And how we feel can greatly impact our effectiveness, energy level, and fulfillment in life. Some of the emotional discipline choices prescribed in this book are rather straightforward and commonly known, such as eating healthy food, exercising, and looking for the positive in difficult circumstances. Unfortunately, all too often these kinds of obvious prescriptions seem to involve a bit too much sacrifice and require too much willpower for us to consistently incorporate them into our lives. However, in this book I will share strategies for approaching these kinds of healthy choices in more reasonable ways so that they can seem less overwhelming and even be experienced more naturally and joyfully.

In addition, many other choices will be described that are probably less common and less familiar (or at least less practiced) to the majority. These include potent strategies such as practicing healthy breathing, purposely feeling your feelings, harnessing the power of silence, and manifesting your life desires. They also include inner jogging through music and humor, choosing the meaning of your feelings, Eastern fitness practices, emotional Kung Fu, finding flow in our work, and having an out-of-ego experience, to name just a few.

I have found the emotional discipline choices included in this book can provide a powerful way to influence the way we feel. My own life has benefited greatly from application of these strategies, many on a regular basis, as needed in my life, and I have observed many benefits enjoyed by others. I am confident that the 25 choices I will share can help you get started with a healthy emotional discipline practice in your own life. They can serve as a foundation for creating customized strategies that address your own unique life circumstances. It is my sincere hope that the ideas in this book will serve you, as they have me, to gain *the power to choose how you feel.*

Acknowledgments

I would like to thank many of my friends and colleagues, from the present and past, who have significantly affected my thinking about self-leadership in ways that helped me to develop the Emotional Discipline perspective, especially the important role of *choice* in determining our personal effectiveness in life and work. They include Hank Sims, Jr., Chris Neck, Greg Stewart, Vikas Anand, Bob Marx, Jim Mancuso, Bob Mitchell, Peter Hom, Frank Shipper, Theodore Levitt, Tom Thompson, Tedd Mitchell, Chris Argyris, Richard Hackman, Denny Gioia, Ed Lawler, Kathi Lovelace, John Newstrom, Mike Beyerlein, Fred Luthans, Bill Glick, John Sheridan, Art Bedeian, Kevin Mossholder, Andy Van de Ven, Hal Angle, Mary Nichols, John Slocum, Mike Mahoney, and my wife and co-author, Karen Manz.

In addition, I thank the University of Massachusetts at Amherst, and especially my Dean and Department Chair in the Isenberg School of Management: Tom O'Brien and Bill

Wooldridge. The Administrative Resources Center, and especially Becky Jerome, have provided me with great support in preparing my book manuscripts over the past few years. Special thanks goes to Charles and Janet Nirenberg, who not only provided the generous gift that made possible my current position as the Nirenberg Professor of Business Leadership but have also been a valued source of inspiration, wisdom, and friendship over the past few years.

I am also very grateful for the "above and beyond the call of duty" encouragement, support, and assistance I received from my editor Steven Piersanti and the very competent, wise, and emotionally disciplined staff at my publisher, Berrett-Koehler. Finally, I express my appreciation to all my other friends, colleagues, and to my extended family who have provided encouragement and support for me and my work through my many emotionally challenging life adventures over the years.

Amherst, Massachusetts   *Charles C. Manz*
                                          January 2003

~~~~~~~~~~~~

The new millennium has brought insider trading, accounting fraud, corrupt leadership, downsizing, corporate restructuring, job insecurity, burst of the technology bubble, hyperturbulent securities markets, natural disasters and wildfires, religious scandals, terrorist attacks, threats of destructive conflict across the globe. . . . Your emotions have been under siege. How will you respond?

Emotional Discipline gives you a Choice.

~~~~~~~~~~~~

~~~~~~~~~~~~

*A Native American boy was talking with his grandfather.
"What do you think about the world situation?" he
asked. The grandfather replied, "I feel like two wolves
are fighting in my heart. One is full of anger and hatred.
The other is full of love, forgiveness, and peace." "Which
one will win?" asked the boy. To which the grandfather
replied, "The one I feed."*

Origin unknown

~~~~~~~~~~~~

Discovering the Power of Emotional Discipline

~ ~ ~ ~ ~

The vast majority of men [and women]
lead lives of quiet desperation.
—Henry David Thoreau

Cecil T. Barkly, the division manager, had just re-
turned to his office after attending what he experi-
enced as a grueling meeting with his subordinate
managers. He felt irritable and exhausted as he gulped
down a cup of coffee and a candy bar and stared at a new
report on his desk. He had stayed up late the previous
night. In fact, he hadn't allowed himself a good night's
sleep in days and always seemed to be eating on the run
to one meeting after another (which was about the only
form of exercise he had taken time for in years).

As he studied the report his face turned red with anger, he clenched his fists. In his unfocused emotional state he misread some data on a graph, thinking that it indicated a negative trend when in fact it showed marked improvement. He sensed that he should take more time to digest the report and to try to put things in perspective before he acted on this new information. But it was too late, his emotions had already taken over and he stormed out of his office, report in hand, and back toward the meeting that he had just left in progress.

When he entered the room, despite an air of excitement in the wake of just having reached a solution to a problem that had haunted the division for months, the group quickly became tensely silent. Barkly felt overwhelming tension in his body and his mind was filled with angry thoughts as he stood and scowled at the group. He was miserable and he was mad and he was going to let this group know how he felt in no uncertain terms!

"I just received information," he began as he thrust the report out in front of him, "that despite our massive attempts to the contrary, managers in this division are still using a directive punitive style of management! You all know our instructions from upstairs to improve employee productivity by adopting a supportive and participative leadership style. You mark my words," he continued, now shaking his fist at the group for emphasis. "You will be more supportive and participative or, dammit, heads are going to roll!"

~ ~ ~ ~ ~

It's true that how you feel can have a dramatic impact on what you do and say and how you experience life in general. The good news is that there are practical ways to gain *The Power to Choose How You Feel*. Do you believe this statement? Can you imagine what it would be like to be able to choose how you feel?

How would you like to be able to make choices that naturally replenish your energy so that you no longer feel drained by work and life? How much value would you place on an ability to change feeling bad into feeling good? How might this ability contribute to your personal effectiveness and fulfillment in life and work? The reality is that much of the time you possess this very ability. All you need is the awareness that you possess this power and effective tools to put it to work. What you need is *Emotional Discipline*.

It is a common tendency to attribute the way we feel to such factors as mood swings, hormone fluctuations, and especially external events. Much of the time it can seem like our quality of life is largely at the mercy of invading feelings that are outside our influence. We hear people say "Sorry, I'm in a lousy mood today," "I feel exhausted," "I can't figure out why I feel so down," or "I don't know what's gotten into me but for some reason I feel great." It's as though we simply have little or no choice regarding how we feel. Emotional Discipline, on the other hand, offers an empowering alternative.

And yet, at least at first glance, the idea of being disciplined about your emotions may seem like a rather unattractive proposition. When I submitted the proposal for this book, a person on staff at my publisher initially had a rather strong and negative reaction. She felt that the idea of emotional discipline was a kind of oxymoron. Her view was that feelings are something to express freely, not to suppress, and that the words "emotion" and "discipline" didn't seem to go together. In fact, the combination left her with an image of something rather stifling and confining. Her view was that "emotional discipline" was certainly not for her.

A couple days later, after a difficult phone call with a business associate, she found herself surprisingly upset and strongly affected by her feelings. As she reflected on her emotional reactions, with a bit of humor thrown in for good measure, she concluded that maybe she needed some emotional discipline after all.

I encourage you, at least for the moment, to let go of whatever initial skepticism or resistance you might feel about the concept of *emotional discipline*. Please allow me to share some of the compelling information surrounding this subject that may open a whole new world for you as it has for me. I ask that you keep an open mind for now to the possibility that it might have something worthwhile to offer you that could help you to live and work with greater personal effectiveness and fulfillment. And I invite you to explore with me the abundant healthy choices that you have available every day that can help you gain *the power to choose how you feel*.

What Is Emotional Discipline?

The simplest, most straightforward answer to this question is that "Emotional Discipline consists of the intentional choices we make to gain the power to choose how we feel." But to define Emotional Discipline with a bit more depth we need to understand the words "emotion" and "discipline."

Emotion. The New World Dictionary defines *emotion* (derived from French and Latin roots meaning to disturb or stir up) as " . . . any specific feeling; any of various complex reactions with both mental and physical manifestations . . . ." Similarly, Salovey and Mayer, authors of the article "Emotional Intelligence," describe emotions as "organized responses, crossing the boundaries of . . . physiological, cognitive, motivational, and experiential systems."[1] Together, these definitions point to "feelings" as the primary vehicle of emotions and suggest that feelings are manifest both physically and mentally.

Consistent with this view, in their recent best-selling book *The Heart of the Soul: Emotional Awareness,* Gary Zukav and Linda Francis describe our experience of emotions as having a physical component, such as pain or discomfort in a location of our body in response to a negative emotion.[2] A positive emotion, on the other hand, will create a pleasant sensation. They explain that these physical feelings are accompanied by thoughts. For example, before making a public speech a person might experience the emotion of anxiety through physical discomfort (such as stomach tightness and/or "butterflies") accompanied by related thoughts ("How did I get myself into this awful situation . . . I'm just going to embarrass myself . . . they'll laugh me out of the room").

And I particularly like the simple description of emotion offered by best-selling author Eckhart Tolle that elegantly captures the spirit of this discussion. He says emotion is "a reflection of your mind in the body."[3]

By viewing emotions as consisting of physical sensations and related mental activity, this means that any given emotion can be identified and examined by studying the sensations in the body (their location, nature, and intensity) and the thoughts that accompany them. For example, imagine that you are swamped with emotion in response to what you perceive as a significant betrayal by a close friend or colleague. Consequently, you notice pain and tightness in your chest accompanied by angry internal self-statements ("How dare she do that . . . after all I've done for her and the way I trusted her . . . she knifed me in the back . . . ").

Discipline. The New World Dictionary defines *discipline* as "a branch of knowledge or learning, . . . training that develops self-control, character, orderliness, . . . submission to authority and control. . . ." If we study these words carefully we can recognize the role of knowledge, learning, and training that broadens the often oversimplified view of discipline. Rather than a stifling, constraining process that limits our choices, discipline can more constructively be viewed in terms of its empowering potential. It can help us transcend the limits of our current learning and overcome disorganized and ineffective responses to powerful forces (such as overpowering emotions) in our life and work experiences.

In her book *Hooked on Feeling Bad*, Joyce Moskowitz similarly describes discipline as "to train or develop, training that corrects, molds and perfects . . . . " And she points out that it stems from the same Latin root as disciple—*discipulus*, which means student—and thus concludes that discipline means "the training of us."[4] In this sense we might think of discipline as a process of self-education and self-training that helps us to enhance our level of effectiveness and the quality of our overall experience in the world.

To reinforce this idea it is helpful to consider the word *disciplines*, which is often associated with spiritual and/or religious practices. For example, the disciplines of meditation, prayer, fasting, study, solitude, and service are usually self-imposed with the intent of experiencing personal growth of mind and spirit. In his classic best-seller *Celebration of Discipline,* Richard Foster argues that disciplines should not be thought of as "dull drudgery aimed at exterminating laughter from the face of the earth . . . the purpose of the disciplines is liberation from the stifling slavery to self-interest and fear."[5]

I will refer to the various strategies for applying emotional discipline included in this book simply as "choices." If you find the concept of "disciplines" helpful, you might think of them as emotional disciplines. Overall, I view *discipline* as a form of self-training and a path to personal growth that stems from entering into (or for those that prefer a bit firmer and more definitive language, submitting to) a process designed to constructively address our experience of life and work.

Emotional Discipline. All this leads to a more comprehensive definition. *Emotional discipline* consists of the various choices you make, both to meet the challenge of current situations as well as to prepare for the future, that provide you with self-training, a path to personal growth, and a repertoire of strategies that you can draw upon as needed, that equip you with *the power to choose how you feel*. This book will offer a specific approach to introducing emotional discipline into your life. It consists of:

~ Selecting (identifying, creating, or customizing) the emotional discipline process that will be used.

~ Working with the process as you encounter work and life challenges that arouse significant feelings.

~ Choosing appropriate strategies (choices) for applying emotional discipline to constructively influence your reactions to situations that trigger significant feelings, as well as to help create future constructive and healthy feelings.

Later in this chapter I will talk more about the various choices that can be made to practice emotional discipline. But first it is important to address the question "why go to the trouble?" That is, what does emotional discipline have to offer that can benefit your life?

The Promise of Emotional Discipline

Why should you bother with emotional discipline in your life and why should you go to the trouble of introducing emotional discipline choices into your daily living? The most simple and direct answer is that they can vastly enhance your experiences of work and life and your overall fulfillment. Making emotional discipline choices not only can enrich your present-moment living and help create a more satisfying and effective future, but can enable you to enjoy a naturally re-energizing lifestyle that can help you avoid feeling depleted and burned out. In addition, by constructively working with and helping to create your feelings, you can vastly contribute to your effectiveness in meeting life's problems, in your interactions and relationships with others, and in growing into your fuller potential.

For example, research has suggested that emotions have the capacity for helping us to successfully face uncertainty, visualize a positive future, and to speed up decision making. Emotions can also help us to bridge between the rational and nonrational, gain a sense of self-relevance, and facilitate personal adaptation and change.[6] One prominent researcher has suggested that emotions represent the "wisdom of the ages" and provide responses to recurrent problems that have withstood the test of time.[7]

Further, significant research has pointed to the many potential benefits of constructive management of emotions. A growing area of research has been grouped under the umbrella term "emotion regulation."[8] Researcher James Gross has commented, "emotional responses can . . . mislead us . . . . When our emotions seem to be ill-matched to a given situation, we frequently try to regulate our emotional responses so that they better serve our goals."[9] And he defines emotion regulation as "The processes by which we influence which emotions we have, when we have them, and how we experience and express them."[10] Research in this area has indicated that effective strategies can be applied for meeting difficult emotional situations that reduce both our negative emotional experiences and our dysfunctional behavioral responses.

Effective regulation of emotions has also been shown to significantly enhance learning. For example, researchers Isen, Daubman, and Nowicki have found that positive emotions can positively impact problem solving while negative emotion inhibits it.[11] It appears that positive emotions engage higher brain mechanisms and enhance processing of information and memory, while negative emotion inhibits higher cognitive functions. For these reasons, as well as evidence that emotions are quite "contagious" and thus easily passed from person to person, Professor Edward Vela argues that teachers should monitor their own emotional state and model and encourage positive emotion for their students.[12] Indeed, a great deal of research supports the value of constructively working with our emotions.

Emotional discipline is worth the trouble because it can be the key to harnessing the power and energy of emotions rather than being wounded and drained by them. And this can help us to have the kind of life and career we've always dreamed of, even if this result stems more from changes in the way we experience life on the inside as opposed to changes in our external life circumstances.

Emotional discipline addresses our most powerful lens for experiencing life—how we feel. Think for a moment. Everything we experience is colored by the way we feel. We all know this at a rational level, but it can be very challenging to identify and implement practical ways of applying this knowledge to positively affect our daily living. When we are in a bad mood, the world can look dark and gloomy. And we can end up acting in ways that alienate others and make our life and work more difficult in the future. When we feel stressed and anxious, everything around us can seem threatening, leaving us psychologically paralyzed and exhausted. We may avoid reasonable and necessary risks for making progress or shy away from great opportunities. If we feel sad or lonely, the world can seem like one big melancholy soap opera robbing us of the joy of the present moment. When we feel tired and apathetic, we may find it difficult to do almost anything at all. And so it goes.

Our life experience is greatly influenced by how we feel, which in turn can play a major role in determining not only our level of satisfaction but how we connect with our work and with other people. Learning the art of *emotional discipline,* and the many tools (*emotional discipline choices*) available for making its potential power a practical personal reality, can create the foundation for an immensely satisfying, fulfilling, energized, and effective life.

Finally, the primary tenet of emotional discipline challenges us to recognize that our emotions are not beyond our control. This holds us accountable for how we feel and how that affects others by means of what we say and do based on those feelings. Such accountability can be not only a good thing but a necessary thing in human relationships. It can help us to better meld together as a society including in our families, friendships, workplaces, neighborhoods, communities, and nations. It offers the potential to help us better live together for the good of one another.

The Key Decisions of Emotional Discipline

Effective practice of Emotional Discipline is founded on four primary decisions. Being truly effective in this practice requires that you decide to commit to:

1. Taking responsibility for how you feel.
2. Doing things now (in the present) that will prepare you (help fill your emotional energy reservoir) for the future.
3. Reacting to emotionally challenging situations in a new, more balanced and healthy way.
4. Making specific choices (applying strategies) to effectively deal with challenges as they arise.

Thus, emotional discipline requires a commitment to preparing for, facing, working with, and responding to emotional challenges constructively. It includes both making choices that equip you to effectively deal with your emotions in the future and addressing immediate issues. Part of Emotional Discipline involves applying a systematic process (such as the one introduced in Chapter 1). But a key part also involves making the decisions above and thereby committing to creating a personal lifestyle in which you can enjoy its benefits on an ongoing basis.

Choices for Gaining in Power to Choose How You Feel

Focusing directly on our emotions in the heat of the moment is not the only way to gain emotional discipline. A variety of choices, which I organize into the categories of mind, body, spirit, and emotional discipline foundations, can help us to calm or manage negative feelings and stimulate positive ones. In practice these choices overlap, but I will examine them separately in this book for the sake of clarity.

Emotional Discipline choices consist of moment to moment, day to day, intentional and proactive strategies we use that can directly or indirectly affect how we feel. They can make a big difference in how we experience events, our effectiveness in life and at work, and our overall sense of fulfillment.

Sometimes the choices involve taking actions that may seem relatively unattractive in the short run but that can make a world of difference in how we feel later. For example, eating a healthy serving of vegetables rather than a thick piece of chocolate cake, or stopping and facing our difficult feelings about a colleague and learning from them rather than losing ourselves in another more appealing but less important task, may not seem like an obvious way to feel better at the time. But, of course, in the long run, we can feel much better and our lives can benefit a great deal if we make these kinds of disciplined choices.

Nevertheless, it is not simply a matter of using disciplined strategies to bolster our willpower or to help us make short-term sacrifices. *Emotional Discipline* also involves discovering the joy of making positive and healthy choices by finding ways to enjoy actions now that will help us to feel even better later. Fresh vegetables cooked creatively can be a culinary delight and taking a brisk walk in a beautiful park, to reflect on thoughts and feelings about a problem we need to address with our colleague, can be a freeing experience.

The amazing thing is that the world is full of healthy and constructive choices that can help us build a life that feels better and that is more effective and fulfilling. And many choices are available to help us more constructively cope and react to our feelings when they are already upon us. The array is as varied as learning techniques for creatively reframing the way we see problems, directly facing and purposely feeling our feelings to lessen their power over us, practicing emotional Kung Fu to put the potency of feelings to work for us, learning some simple and effective meditation techniques, and applying the power of silence.

This book offers 25 specific emotional discipline choices, or ways to gain *The Power to Choose How You Feel,* including selecting an overall process that serves as the foundation for emotional discipline. For the most part these practical strategies are relatively simple, well known, and have proven to be very effective for many people. They represent a solid beginning set of alternatives that you can expand upon and adapt to your needs. The specific strategies (choices) are designed to help uplift the way you feel about your work and life by equipping you to better respond to your feelings in the present and help you constructively shape them for the future. Together these practical strategies can establish a solid beginning repertoire of choices for bringing the many benefits of emotional discipline into your experience.

As stated previously, the various choices/strategies offered are divided into four areas: emotional discipline foundations, mind, body, and spirit. Hopefully you will find some of these practical strategies especially helpful for your particular life circumstances. Feel free to "jump around" in your reading after you read Chapters 1 and 2. Those two chapters address selection of a fundamental emotional discipline multi-step process and the key characteristics of emotional discipline, and thus should be read first. The strategies in the rest of the chapters don't need to be read in any particular order.

Strategies also work across more than the application area they are grouped under. For example, you may find some of the techniques for addressing the mind are very helpful with issues of the spirit or vice versa. You may also discover that certain strategies for enhancing the way your body feels also calm your mind or that better coping with your troubling thoughts relieves all kinds of symptoms in your body. As already pointed out, emotions are manifested as physical sensations in the body (such as butterflies in the stomach or tightness in the chest) along with various patterns of thought (for example, worrisome mental images or euphoric internal self-talk). Also, many believe our feelings are the primary language of the spirit. For example, the information about what is truly right for our lives may be contained more in an inner wisdom that is communicated through intuition and feelings as opposed to conscious rational analytical thinking.

Please experiment and adapt the suggested emotional discipline choices to your own particular needs and situation. You can combine strategies or use only the parts that resonate with you. I hope the practical choices contained in this book will also inspire you to create some of your own that are specifically customized to your unique needs and perspective. Think of this book as a living document that you can help create, mold, and incorporate into your life and work as you see fit.

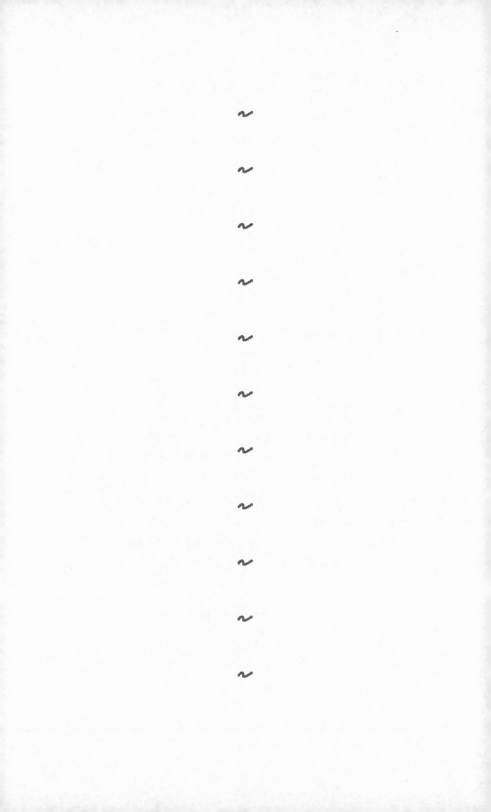

Our emotions wield a powerful force that greatly affects the quality of our life experience. Being able to honestly face our emotions and to really be with them is essential for living a full life. And being able to manage our responses to them well, and make choices that foster the creation of healthy emotions for the future, is the key to living effectively.

~~~~~~~~~~~

.

Part One

Emotional Discipline Foundations

~ ~ ~ ~ ~

By starving emotions we become humorless, rigid, and stereotyped; by repressing them we become literal, reformatory and holier-than-thou; encouraged they perfume life; discouraged, they poison it.

—Joseph Collins[13]

Choice 1

Create Your Emotional Discipline Process

~~~~~

If I had my life to live over again, I would have made a rule to read some poetry and listen to some music at least once a week; for perhaps the parts of my brain now atrophied would have thus been kept active through use. The loss of these tastes is a loss of happiness, and may possibly be injurious to the intellect, and more probably to the moral character, by enfeebling the emotional part of our nature.

—Charles Darwin[14]

The first and most important emotional discipline choice is to select an overall process for applying emotional discipline. Ultimately you will need a process that is designed specifically for you. This chapter will introduce the five key components or steps that need to be addressed in the process that you create to fit your specific needs. To help you get started, a sample of a complete process for practicing emotional discipline will be presented along with a case example that illustrates how it might be used.

The five components or steps of a complete emotional discipline process were derived from several key sources. They are partly based on the work I have been pursuing with colleagues on the topic of self-leadership over the last twenty years.[15] This source of input draws upon my personal knowledge gained from research, consulting, and teaching experiences. Over the past two decades I have had the opportunity to study and facilitate learning for thousands of people regarding their self-leadership practices, including the incorporation of positive discipline in their work and lives. Beyond this direct input and experience I drew upon several other key sources that I have found to be particularly helpful in the literature on personal growth and improvement. I have personally tried many of the strategies that these sources suggest (and all of the ones included in this book) and observed them in many others.

First, I will describe in detail the five key components or steps of a complete emotional discipline process and provide a sample process that incorporates all of them. Learning these steps, adapting them to your specific circumstances (customizing them to your individual needs), and using them as a source of inspiration to create your own emotional discipline process, is key. It represents the foundation for, and the first of, the 25 *choices* (strategies) that make up the primary content of this book.

Then I will provide a concrete case example that demonstrates how the process might be applied to a specific challenging situation. Later, in the chapter on Emotional Intelligence (Chapter 4), some of the books that were helpful with the development of the process and that can further add to your knowledge for effective practice of emotional discipline are listed. I recommend that you consider reading some of these books for additional information and guidance on the emotional discipline process.

Five Components or Steps for Practicing Emotional Discipline

The effective overall practice of emotional discipline as a lifestyle commitment includes five specific components or steps. Together they can be applied to meet current life challenges as well as to help develop your capacity for meeting emotionally challenging situations in the future. Ultimately they are founded on the powerful idea of CHOICE—choosing how you feel through the application of an overall multistep process and specific strategies (emotional discipline choices) to meet immediate challenges. Here are the components or steps:

1. **Cause**—identify the immediate cause of your emotions.

2. **Body**—assess the location and intensity of your physical reactions.

3. **Mind**—identify the thoughts and beliefs that accompany your physical reactions.

4. **Spirit**—note what part of yourself is being revealed in
   your response to your current circumstances.

5. **Choice**—make an emotional discipline choice and
   apply it for constructively dealing with your immediate challenge.

The key, at least in the beginning, is to incorporate all
five of these into your emotional discipline efforts as you
encounter circumstances that trigger your emotions. It is
usually very helpful to do your initial work in writing.
Writing out your thoughts as you work with the five steps
provides a special kind of discipline and can reveal deeper
insights than just running through them in your mind.

Eventually, your own customized emotional discipline
process should become almost automatic and second nature and will not require that all the steps be used for every
emotion-filled circumstance. For example, you may reach
the "mind" focused stage and naturally find yourself drawing upon an appropriate emotional discipline choice, such
as mental reframing, that addresses your immediate needs.
In effect this represents automatically jumping to the final
"choice" part of the process as you become more experienced and effective in applying emotional discipline. Or
some circumstances (particularly ones you have encountered in the past) may automatically prompt your use of a

specific choice without needing to work through any of the first four steps.

Also, one other point of clarification needs to be made at the outset. In Step 4 of the process (as well as Part Four of this book) the word *spirit* is used, which has been assigned many meanings over the years. In this book I refer to spirit less in terms of its religious and supernatural implications, and more as that part of who we are that represents our best and most constructive self. This view is relatively consistent with many writers and speakers who make the distinction between our ego (which generally includes our more fearful, closed, selfish, and destructive self) and our spirit (which usually reflects our more caring, open, trusting, and constructive self).

Some dictionaries include more than a dozen different meanings for *spirit*. Some portions of the definition contained in the New American Webster Dictionary that capture best how I am using the term here include "The nature of a person . . . vivacity; optimism . . . the essence or real meaning." In this book, spirit is generally used to indicate that part of ourselves that we recognize as the best that is in us and, from an optimistic stance, the more accurate reflection of who we really are.

A Sample of a Complete Emotional Discipline Process

What follows is a complete 5-step emotional discipline process. This sample process is offered to help you get started. It is possible that you may even find that this specific process adequately addresses your particular needs and that you can begin to use it to meet your own life challenges. More likely you will need to create a customized process, and use the one offered here as a source of insight and inspiration for creating an approach that is better suited to your own circumstances.

For example, if health issues are especially prominent in your life, you will probably need to create a process that emphasizes constructive ways of addressing your physical needs. If on the other hand, you are struggling with painful mental issues due to a recent loss of some kind, the mind part of the process would receive more emphasis. The 5-step process that follows represents a comprehensive generic approach to practicing emotional discipline.

1. What is the *Cause*?

Identify the issue or event provoking the feelings. What has happened that has triggered significant emotion for you? Have you encountered a setback in your life or work, a disagreement with someone else, a troubling thought or realization in your mind, or some other circumstance? This might be a long-term issue that keeps recurring or it might be an unexpected one-time event. Step 1 involves specifically pinpointing whatever it is that is stirring up feelings that you feel a need to address.*

---

*Note that the "Cause" part of the process is intended to focus on immediate salient events or issues that are triggering your emotional responses and notable feelings. It is not, however, generally meant to address deep psychological problems, such as those that might stem from serious childhood traumas or unconscious or repressed psychological issues, that may require psychotherapy or other professional treatment.

2. Focus on Your *Body*

Scan your body. Determine the location of your physical sensations and whether they are uncomfortable or pleasant. Where specifically are you having the physical feelings? Are you feeling tightness in your chest, butterflies in your stomach, a pleasant flowing warmth throughout your entire body, tingling down your spine, or some other physical sensation? Pinpoint the location of the physical feelings and whether you are experiencing them as pleasing or painful.

Rate your physical feelings. How do you rate the physical feelings you have pinpointed on a scale ranging from –10 for very negative (uncomfortable/painful) to +10 for very positive (comfortable/enjoyable). If, as a result of a heated argument, you have a strong unpleasant knotted feeling in the pit of your stomach, accompanied by rather severe tightness in your chest, you might rate the sensation as a –8 or –9. If, on the other hand, as you sit under a palm tree on a tropical beach with a warm light breeze gently caressing your hair, you are experiencing deep calmness and muscle relaxation along with a wave of contented pleasure throughout your entire body, you might rate this sensation as a +8 or +9.

3. Focus on Your *Mind*

Identify your thoughts and/or images that accompany the feelings. What thoughts are going through your head as you experience these physical sensations? What internal statements (e.g., "this argument is awful . . . he is being

terribly rude and unreasonable . . . this kind of stress could
ruin my health . . .") and/or mental pictures (images of the
other person later saying things to discredit you behind
your back . . . seeing yourself in an ambulance as a result of
having a stroke or heart attack . . .) are running through
your mind?

Identify your beliefs that underlie your thoughts. What beliefs
do you hold that are laying the foundation for your mental
and physical reactions? For example, do you believe that
things should always go smoothly and that all problems are
bad, people should not argue, strong feelings are bad for
you, it is important to always keep your feelings tightly
under control, when anyone disagrees with you it represents an attack? Pinpoint what you specifically believe that
forms the foundation for your stance and reaction to the
situation or event.

4. Focus on Your *Spirit*

*Determine what part of yourself is being revealed and what
part is being hidden.* We tend to have different noteworthy
parts of who we are that are more or less engaged at different times. Some of these parts we tend to like and value
and others we don't. For example, in your response to this
issue or event, are you acting from a state of openness, caring, and love? Or are you acting from a state of fear, defensiveness, and hostility? As you work with this process
across different situations, try to become aware of the different aspects of yourself that you live and act from in different situations. Also, work toward gaining a better sense

of those parts of yourself you would like to have more revealed and activated and those that you would not.

5. Make a *Choice*

Choose your actions and reactions (your emotional discipline strategies). The greatest value of emotional discipline is in its potential to increase your power to choose, and most notably, to choose how you feel. In response to the issue or event that you have pinpointed, how would you like to be able to respond? What actions and reactions (in terms of physical sensations, thinking, and action strategies) would you like to have? More specifically, what emotional discipline *choices* have you built into your repertoire that you can draw upon to constructively address your current feelings and to help you create constructive future feelings? What choices can help you to experience and live from your more constructive, effective, and empowered self a greater amount of the time and in more situations?

An Example of the Process in Action

(Note: The following case was written to illustrate the complete 5-step process, but it is inspired by actual events.)

The founder and beloved leader of an emerging service-oriented software firm unexpectedly passed away about three weeks ago. Since that time the organization has been largely paralyzed and ineffective and experiencing a business-threatening downturn as a result. Today the remaining 21 members of the management team of this rapidly growing enterprise have gathered to support one another and to begin to

sort out the implications of their former leader's death and
how they can proceed from here. This is the first time they
have been together in the primary meeting room at their main
corporate office without their deceased leader. No specific
agenda was set for the meeting. Mostly, some key members of
the management team felt a time was needed to get everyone
together in one place to begin the process of moving forward.

A sense of despair filled the room. Some people had tears
in their eyes and others spoke of the deep sadness they felt and
their anxieties about the future of their firm. Kris Woltuf's initial reaction had been much like that of the other managers.
She was overwhelmed by difficult feelings, including deep sadness and anxiety, when she first heard the news. She felt an uncomfortable tightness in her chest and a knot in her stomach.
In her mind she focused on all they had lost by the passing of
their very compassionate and inspiring leader. She was not
able to think clearly and was ineffective in her job. And she
was unable to be the way she wanted for her husband and two
children, especially when significant family challenges arose.
She just seemed to lack the strength and will to be fully present
in her life. That is, until she made a conscious choice to work
with the emotional discipline process.

~ ~ ~ ~ ~

For *Step 1*, it was easy for her to identify the triggering
event as the loss of her friend and leader. She then pinpointed the primary location of the physical discomfort as
residing in her chest and stomach in *Step 2*. And she felt
the intensity of the physical sensations was pretty high.

Consequently, she rated the physical discomfort as a negative 6 on the physical feelings rating scale.

Next, in *Step 3* she identified her corresponding thoughts. She recorded on a note pad some of her more prominent internal statements. These included, "This is an absolute tragedy to lose such a wonderful and inspiring man" . . . "The firm will be lost without his leadership" . . . "Why even bother with our work." And she noted some of her mental images such as picturing a sense of hopelessness and despair hanging over the company for years to come and even eventual bankruptcy for the firm.

She also recognized some of her underlying beliefs including the following. "Good people shouldn't die, especially unexpectedly." "The entire strength of the firm was tied up in one single person who is now gone." And "extreme situations like this are entirely destructive and beyond our ability to constructively respond to."

Recognizing these dominant thoughts and beliefs helped her with *Step 4*. She recognized that she was mostly responding to the situation from a part of herself that was fearful and that felt and acted like a helpless victim. She knew that acting from this part of herself would not enable her to be of much help to others who were affected by the death nor to effectively perform her job or to be supportive of her family the way she wanted.

Consequently, for *Step 5*, she made some specific choices for applying emotional discipline to turn things around. For example, in addition to choosing to *work through the 5-step emotional discipline process*, she chose to allow herself to really *feel her feelings*. Up to that point she

had tried to avoid her feelings as much as possible. She had
been largely tuning out life as an unconscious way of avoiding feeling any more than she had to. Now she moved in
closer to her feelings and faced them squarely. It was rather
frightening and uncomfortable at first, but she practiced
deep *abdominal breathing* to help her calm herself. As she
began to recognize the location and nature of her physical
sensations and the kinds of thoughts and beliefs that were
attached to them, her new awareness seemed to lessen the
intensity of her emotions. It was as though she had pointed
a flashlight into a dark eerie corner of a room. When she
could more clearly see and understand the nature of her
feelings, their power over her was greatly diminished.

And she made some healthy choices to care for her
body in a way that lifted how she felt physically. Since she
was finding it especially difficult to initiate new activities in
her current state of mind, she kept these choices very simple. She made a conscious commitment to get some *exercise* at least once every day. Mostly she took 20 to 30
minutes at lunch time to walk around the small lake and
through the wooded grounds of the office park of her company's building. Other times she used an exercise bike or
worked out with a yoga video that had been collecting dust
on a shelf at home. And she made a conscious choice to *cut
down on sweets and caffeine* which she knew adversely affected her mood, especially when she was under stress.

She also used *mental reframing* of the event. Instead of
viewing the situation as a seemingly endless catastrophe
calling for mourning and suffering, she chose to view it as a
time to be grateful for all that the leader had brought to her

and others and the way he had enriched their lives. She also viewed it as a chance to carry on his legacy. Essentially she had practiced *emotional Kung Fu* by redirecting her emotional energy to help the situation work for her rather than against her. This caused her to begin sharing many positive memories with her colleagues and parts of the inspiring vision that had helped launch the company.

As she did this in the current gathering, she noticed that the tone of the whole room began to gradually turn around. Soon others were also telling positive stories about what the leader had done for them and what they had accomplished together. And they began to reconnect with the mission and purpose they had felt under the inspiration of their leader. As this process unfolded, the beginning of a healing process had begun. The managers, for the first time since their leader's death, focused on how they had in fact been left with a great deal of strength, inspiration, and vision. They also began to see that they were very capable of successfully carrying on together.

Concluding Comments

Now I invite you to read about, try out, adapt, and add to the emotional discipline choices contained in the following chapters. Some of these strategies especially match up with a particular step of the process. Note that the four parts of the book are divided into emotional discipline foundations, mind, body, and spirit. The latter three of these correspond with the key parts of the emotional discipline process that was introduced in this chapter.

Also remember that any of the emotional discipline choices can be applied directly during any step of the emotional discipline process. Again, this is essentially jumping to the final *"choice"* stage of the process when you find yourself ready to do so. Sometimes working through all five steps of the process (or all the steps of your customized version) can be very helpful. Other times it will be obvious that a specific choice is just what you seem to need after only working part way through the steps. And most importantly, as you incorporate these kinds of constructive emotional discipline choices into your life and work you will increasingly gain in your ongoing capacity to have *the power to choose how you feel.*

Choice 2

Learn the Key Characteristics of Emotional Discipline

~~~~~

Your emotions are your inner guidance system. . . . You have, within you, the power to create a life of joy, abundance, and health, or you have the same ability to create a life filled with stress, fatigue, and disease. With very few exceptions, the choice is yours.

—Christiane Northrup[16]

He did it again. *Phil Jackson, one of the most successful coaches in the history of basketball, led the LA Lakers to the NBA championship in 2002. In 12 seasons as a head coach of the LA Lakers and Chicago Bulls, he has now led his teams to nine NBA championships. During the 2002 playoffs, the Lakers found themselves significantly down in crucial games as well as behind two games to three in the series against the Sacramento Kings. Meanwhile, most of the time Jackson appeared relatively unruffled and unemotional, and the team seemed to possess a surprising calm confidence, even when things looked most bleak.*

While other coaches are frequently observed intensely shouting directions and commands to players, Jackson is usually sitting quietly on the bench watching the flow of the action rather than trying to control it. His style has been described this way, "Mostly he sits with his fingers interlocked over crossed knees, his head tilted back and angled toward the action. If he is slightly agitated he'll start to bend forward, his mouth opening . . . but he rarely looses his cool." Ron Harper, who played guard under him at the Chicago Bulls, has said, "He knows how to talk to guys . . . he don't holler and scream . . . but he's far from a pushover."[17]

Jackson, who formerly coached the Chicago Bulls to six NBA championships in nine seasons while achieving a best in NBA history .738 winning percentage in regular season play, frequently displayed rather unusual coaching strategies during his tenure. For example, in one game, at the time Chicago Bull star Scottie Pippen refused to enter the game with 1.8 seconds left. After the game Jackson closed the locker room door and said to the team, "What happened has hurt us. Now you have to work this out. You've got two minutes to get together, to talk softly among yourselves."

Jackson is something of an enigma. A self-proclaimed Zen Christian, he is a highly competitive individual and yet works with his players to establish a spirit of self-less team play, including frequent use of the team (not star) oriented strategy known as the triangle offense. Jackson's distinctive coaching methods have combined a variety of techniques such as meditation, visualization, and a focus on mindfulness, oneness, and attunement.[18]

He's unpredictable. He's been known to call time-outs when you don't expect them and not to call them when you do. He doesn't yell or scream in the tradition of legendary successful coaches in highly competitive sports. When he's angry at his team he's more likely to stand up, stuff his hands in his pockets, and just give the players a good hard look. When there is a problem within the team, as the Pippen example suggests, he may well drop the problem in the players' lap to solve for themselves. And he has the best winning percentage of any NBA coach in history.

~ ~ ~ ~ ~

As a coach, Phil Jackson could be described as a model and teacher of Emotional Discipline, which like the intriguing aspects of his coaching style, has a number of rather unique and even paradoxical characteristics. In this chapter some of these key characteristics of emotional discipline will be addressed directly. It is important that you make a choice to learn about these key characteristics.

Being aware of them can better prepare you to practice emotional discipline effectively and, perhaps like Phil Jackson,
help keep you unruffled in the heat of your emotionally challenging situations in life. Specifically, emotional
discipline has several key requirements, paradoxes, and
limitations.

The Key Requirements of Emotional Discipline

Emotional discipline does not appear spontaneously out of
thin air. For most people it is not something that will occur
automatically simply because they decide they want it to be
part of their lives. There are some key requirements to establish constructive and meaningful emotional discipline.
What are these requirements? Consider the following.

~**Commitment and Motivation to Engage in the
Process.** Developing and practicing emotional discipline requires a sincere desire to engage in the process
and a motivation to increase in ability to work with
and choose how you feel. Unless you have real motivation and commitment to pursue emotional discipline, your attempts are not likely to succeed.

~**An Effective Process to Work With and Enter Into.**
The backbone of emotional discipline consists of the
process that you create and use to work with your
feelings. In the previous chapter a multistep process
was described in detail. The process was offered as
one possible way to begin a practice of emotional discipline. You may, however, prefer a much different

version that you believe will better fit your personal needs. Nevertheless, the five fundamental components or steps described in Chapter 1 need to be addressed somehow in your emotional discipline process. These include: cause–body–mind–spirit–choice.

~ **Trust in the Process and Persistence in Using It.** For emotional discipline to be firmly established you must possess confidence in the process you apply and consequently persist in applying it. If you lack the trust necessary to consistently use the emotional discipline process you have identified, even if you do manage to get yourself to try it out once in a while as an experiment, you will lack the persistent follow-through required to really make it work. Thus, if you are not satisfied with the process you have selected, you need to modify it or replace it until you find one that you can faithfully commit to.

~ **Effective Emotional Discipline Choices to Choose From.** An essential part of emotional discipline is an effective set of alternative *choices* (strategies to work with and help create your feelings) to apply as you encounter challenges and issues that trigger your feelings at work and in life.

~ **A Spirit of Flexibility and Adaptability to Refine the Emotional Discipline Process.** Finally, you need to bring an experimental and creative mind-set to your practice of emotional discipline. There are many possible processes (such as the one outlined in Chapter 1) you can follow to work with the physical sensations and thoughts that make up your emotions. And you can choose from many potential emotional discipline strategies (such as the 25 choices offered in this book) to help you cope with, respond to, and in general choose your feelings. Flexibility and adaptability are crucial for enabling you to optimally create a process that fits your particular needs and circumstances.

The Paradoxes of Emotional Discipline

Along with these key requirements, emotional discipline also entails a good dose of paradox. Here are some primary paradoxes of emotional discipline:

~ **The seeming restrictions and constraints of practicing discipline can provide a significant new level of freedom.** Engaging in the emotional discipline process, which on the surface may appear to involve giving up a degree of immediate choice, can actually free you from the bounds of fear and other debilitating feelings that constrain your range of choices and ability to freely live.

~ **Submission to (entering into) the emotional discipline process adds to your power rather than taking it away.** As you learn to master the constructive processing of your feelings and the application of various emotional discipline choices, you empower yourself for more positive experiences and for new degrees of personal effectiveness, particularly in the face of emotion-laden challenges.

~The sacrifice of immediate pleasure and gratification implied by the notion of **making disciplined choices can actually increase the level of joy and pleasure that you derive from your experiences.** By increasing your awareness of and learning how to respond to, work with, and create your feelings, you are able to enjoy a new level of power to choose how you feel.

~Discipline, which you might ordinarily associate with rigid adherence and lack of flexibility, in this case, requires openness to adapting and refining the process. That is, **emotional discipline, while requiring a commitment to consistent practice, also requires a kind of adaptability and flexibility** that allows for continuous refinement and customization of the process to your particular needs and circumstances.

~Undertaking the **development of emotional discipline requires a certain amount of discipline.** In other words, to increase in emotional discipline you need to bring some discipline to the process at the outset. It may not require a lot, since the structure contained in the 5-step process provides a level of built-in procedural discipline, but it does require some to initiate and follow through.

Some Cautions and Limitations

It is important to make clear that Emotional Discipline is not about suppression of feelings and living a cold stilted life. Being emotionally disciplined is not a simple matter of constraining your emotions through force of will and numbing your reactions to situations that would otherwise affect you. The irony is that emotional discipline can actually free you to more fully experience your whole range of feelings in a thoughtful, reflective, and meaningful way. It can free you from emotional chaos and from the natural tendency to recoil and constrain your feelings out of fear of losing control, and it can introduce a sense of emotional power and joy into your life.

To enjoy these possible healthy and constructive benefits, keep these limitations and cautions in mind as you begin to apply emotional discipline. First, *it is not a process for avoiding significant issues in your life that need to be addressed.* If you have significant challenges that need your attention emotional discipline should not be used as a way to avoid the important work that needs to take place. This work may be in the form of repairing relationships through difficult but meaningful communication, implementing changes that need to take place in your work and career, making lifestyle adjustments that promote recovery from an illness or an unhealthy life pattern, or taking a good hard look at yourself and doing the work to develop your own life purpose or vision and goals. Emotional discipline is not the application of techniques that provide a short-term elevation of mood in order to avoid the important issues you need to address in your life.

Second, emotional discipline *is not a way to stuff your feelings.* Feelings in themselves are neither good nor bad, but they do need to be recognized as an important part of life. Studying your feelings can help you learn more about yourself. Honestly facing your feelings (not dwelling on them but honestly recognizing and acknowledging them) can actually lessen their power over you, whereas suppressing them may cause them to become distorted and increase their power. For example, research has found that suppression of our reactions to emotion not only tends to be less effective for alleviating negative emotional experiences than strategies that acknowledge and work with the emotion (such as reappraising a difficult situation), but it also tends to impair memory.[19]

In fact, one specific area of research addresses the idea of emotional labor. More specifically, studies have examined the physical and psychological toll of work situations that require employees to display positive emotions even when they are feeling very poorly.[20] For example, many service jobs, such as sales clerks in retail stores or wait staff in restaurants, require employees to respond to customers, even very rude ones, in a cheerful and courteous manner. If an employee is worried about an ill child at home or has just been treated very badly by a manager or customer, the effort required to project false emotions can have a significant detrimental impact on the person. Emotional discipline is not intended as a means for falsely manipulating emotions to project an artificial image to others. On the other hand, emotional discipline can help create a hardiness and capacity to handle potentially provoking situations without the experience of destructive emotional reactions and thus largely remove the need to project false impressions.

Third, be aware that *working with emotions can be self-deceiving at times.* By mastering some tools for managing your emotions, you may find that you can feel better for a while, only to discover later that you were involved in self-deception. For example, if you apply mental strategies that only temporarily distract you from facing challenges that need to be faced, over time you may well find the situation actually gets worse. Again, if real problems exist that need your attention and effort, a healthy emotional discipline process requires choosing to constructively face the issues for the longer term and not just making choices that help you create a temporary illusion so that you can feel better in the moment.

Fourth, you also need to be aware that *the process of emotional discipline, and the various choices it contains, may at times seem rather simple and perhaps even obvious and trivial.* Don't underestimate its power. Many healthy choices are available to us that can make a tremendous difference in our lives, and they may be as simple as taking an enjoyable walk, eating an extra vegetable each day, taking time to listen to relaxing music, regularly meditating for 10 minutes, or practicing observing heated situations rather than reacting to them. Unfortunately, you (like myself and most everyone else) are probably aware of many simple and seemingly obvious healthy choices but often do not make them. They may simply require just a little extra willpower, a slightly different focus in your thinking, or a new habit that isn't naturally there. The emotional discipline choices contained in this book are designed to be simple, straightforward, and very capable of being built into your lifestyle. Together they can empower you to gain the power to choose how you feel.

A limitation of this book is that it *does not directly address differences in the challenges that arise based on physiology and life circumstances.* For example, women and men may face differing challenges based on hormonal and other physiological differences, social pressures, and work/life demands. People at different life stages, such as early adulthood vs. retirement years, are faced with differing emotional pressures that need to be addressed. And some people may have special conditions such as Asperger's Syndrome (a form of autism), in which people cannot effectively read emotions in themselves or others, or Seasonal Affective Disorder (a condition caused by winter and a lack of sunlight). But even in these cases a person can *choose* to partner with others who are particularly in tune with emotions or add therapeutic lighting and plan annual vacation time to sunny climates during winter months. All this is part of the reason that it is important that individuals be aware of their unique life challenges and customize their emotional discipline process and choices to their own specific circumstances.

Another related limitation is that *this book does not provide an in-depth discussion of the complex origins of emotion,* which, while widely studied, remain largely a mystery in medical and psychological science. Clearly both biological and psychological factors are involved, but the primary forces and how they are combined for each unique individual are very complex. Childhood trauma and genetic influences are just a couple of the many potent elements that help shape emotion. For example, researchers at the National Institute of Health have recently released results

of a study that links a specific gene to the activity of the
amygdala, a portion of the brain that controls the fear response.[21] The findings suggest that those persons with a
shorter form of this gene are more susceptible to anxiety
and a stronger response to fearful stimuli. This book focuses on constructively assessing and working with emotion but not untangling the mysteries of the roots of
emotion for a given person, which to be fully understood
would likely require psychotherapy and medical study.

And this raises the final limitation: *Emotional discipline is not intended as a substitute for professional help when
it is needed.* The choices offered in this book are powerfully
capable of helping you to feel and be better in your life and
work. But they do not replace professional support, treatment, and help from a competent psychiatrist, psychologist, or other counselor when it is required for more
serious cases.

Despite these limitations and cautions, the practical
strategies contained in this book are designed to help us
better cope and work with feeling bad. By getting in touch
with difficult feelings, and better handling and managing
the effects they have on our lives, we can vastly elevate our
entire experience of life and our personal effectiveness.
This book also contains many useful prescriptions for increasing the quantity and quality of the moments we feel
good. Certainly parts of life are tragic and contain great
suffering, such as when a loved one is lost or in the experience of a severe illness (physical or mental) or disease.
Significant life changes, due to aging, job loss, relationship
breakdowns, or moving to a new home, can sometimes

seem so overwhelming that having the power to affect how we feel can seem well beyond our grasp. Nevertheless, for most of us, much more often than we realize, we can and do significantly influence the way we feel as we live and work. That is what this book is all about—using *Emotional Discipline* to gain *The Power To Choose How You Feel*.

Choice 3

Choose the Meaning
of Your Feelings

*We know the truth not only by reason
but also by the heart.*[22]

—Blaise Pascal

The dot-com collapse of 2000–2001 had a devastating effect on the U.S. and world markets, and the fortunes, careers, and quality of life for many, many people. Surely this economic crash could leave only a wake of despair, hopelessness, demoralization, and other such painful feelings. Right?

Not according to Steven Levy, author of a cover story in *Newsweek* titled *"How the Bust Saved Silicon Valley"*. Large bold letters at the beginning of the article proclaim "it was the best thing to happen to this high-tech crucible."[23] Levy argues that the bust, which worked to remove much of the reckless excess that characterized the boom, may have been a good thing for the future of technology. He suggests that, among other things, it will produce a leaner and meaner, highly innovative, prudent, next phase. Very smart people (who lost their jobs) became willing to work creatively for reasonable pay and with commitment to the ideas they are pursuing, as opposed to focusing more on the riches they could win. After viewing the situation from Levy's perspective, it is hard not to feel a bit upbeat, optimistic, and downright hopeful. And it is hard not to realize that, even in the face of what appear to be very trying circumstances, we can exert considerable influence over how we feel.

As you examine various choices you can make to have greater power over how you feel, none is more potent than purposely choosing the feelings you experience and their meaning for your life. At the end of this chapter concrete descriptions are provided for what I call old and new views of feeling good and feeling bad. And the box on the following page provides a small sample of the many feelings that can powerfully affect your experience of life. It is not intended to be an exhaustive list of all the feelings that impact how you experience events, but it does make clear that feelings are a pervasive part of your life.* It also accentuates the powerful implications of choosing how you feel.

It is useful to ponder and add to this list. Consider how each of these feelings affects you and how differently you will experience life when you are under their influence. For example, if you feel tired, overwhelmed, and insecure, you will experience life in a dramatically different way than if you feel courageous, inspired, and confident. And again, the good news is that you can to a significant degree choose how you feel.

Feelings are powerful forces in our lives, often triggered by our life experiences. Yet we are the ultimate leaders of the way we experience life, regardless of our circumstances. This lesson was made all too clear by Viktor Frankl in his classic book *Man's Search for Meaning*.[24] Frankl vividly depicted life for Jews in a Nazi concentration camp during World War II and how the choice each

---

*While the primary umbrella concept of this book—*emotional discipline*—centers on emotion, in a broader sense "feelings" (some of which, such as feeling "tired," do not necessarily correspond with a specific emotion) are a key consideration. In this book, "feelings" are viewed as largely overlapping with emotions but are more heavily weighted toward sensations in the body, whereas emotions (which are sometimes considered to be synonymous with feelings) are manifest more in a combination of physical and mental components. Nevertheless, many feelings (feeling tired, sick, stressed) that do not represent a specific emotion, heavily influence and are influenced by emotions. And they are an important part of an overall effort to constructively introduce healthy discipline into our lives to enable us to experience greater effectiveness and fulfillment.

Some of the Feelings that Affect Your Experience of Life

Think about the times when you feel:

angry	amused	contented	tired
ashamed	cranky	depressed	afraid
helpless	egotistical	worried	lazy
timid	righteous	enthusiastic	nervous
strong	bored	resentful	inspired
expectant	sick	greedy	lustful
skeptical	infatuated	threatened	mellow
eager	overwhelmed	nauseated	impressed
creative	delighted	embarrassed	lovable
energetic	insecure	calm	enlightened
corrupted	vital	proud	loved
determined	hopeful	balanced	vibrant
terrified	courageous	noble	pure
superior	called	magnificent	redeemed
cynical	confused	apathetic	euphoric
sulky	compassionate	frustrated	disoriented
insecure	confident	vulnerable	strange

GOOD

prisoner made in responding to the terrible conditions affected not only their everyday experience but their very survival. Those that found purpose and meaning in the midst of their hardship were uplifted despite their dire circumstances and were far more likely to survive and even thrive.

This sense of meaning, the "why" for their existence, was displayed in ways as simple as giving scraps of bread and a little encouragement to other prisoners in need. One interpretation is that they chose to feel needed, compassionate, and loving as opposed to feeling despair, hopelessness, and futility. The ones who chose the more hopeful and serving response experienced a dramatically different world from those who reacted to the same difficult circumstances by simply giving up hope.

This lesson suggests one of the keys to better understanding and to beginning to benefit from the powerful insight that you can choose how you feel. That is, you can choose to see your feelings in a whole new light and thereby intentionally choose the meaning of your feelings. In this spirit the next page contains old and new views of what it means to feel bad and good. Please consider these viewpoints carefully. They are a useful starting point to embrace choosing the way you feel. Which box do you choose? That is what this book is all about—embracing and working with the reality that *how you feel is a* **Choice**.

"FEELING" BAD

Old View: Negative and painful emotional energy, caused by factors outside ourselves, that
☞   Deflates immediate experience
☞   Represents a source of inner turmoil that is out of our control
☞   Is a mysteriously unpredictable and threatening force.

"FEELING" GOOD

Old View: Positive and enjoyable emotional energy, caused by factors outside ourselves, that:
☞   Elevates our immediate experience
☞   Represents a source of inner pleasure that is sought and valued
☞   Is a mysteriously unpredictable and seductive force.

"FEELING" BAD OR GOOD

New View: A state of being that results from who we choose to be on a daily basis and that:
☞   Arises from forces contained in our mind, body, emotions, and spirit
☞   Forms a powerfully sensitive lens that greatly affects the way we experience life
☞   Is a most colorful and interesting part of life that we can learn to collaborate with.

Choice 4

Increase Your Emotional Intelligence (EQ)

Something we were withholding made us weak,
until we found out that it was ourselves.

—Robert Frost

I t is no longer surprising news that rational "book smart" intelligence is not enough to live successfully. Our hearts as well as our brains are critical. In fact, it is EQ (emotional intelligence) rather than IQ that has become the recent center of attention for those wishing to be more effective in their work and life.

Daniel Goleman popularized the concept of emotional intelligence (EQ) in his best-selling book.[25] According to Goleman,

> emotional intelligence refers to the capacity for recognizing our own feelings and those of others, for motivating ourselves, and for managing emotions well in ourselves and in our relationships. It describes abilities distinct from, but complementary to, academic intelligence, the purely cognitive capacities measured by IQ.[26]

Research suggests that EQ is every bit as important as IQ (intelligence quotient) for determining our effectiveness. It can help us to be more perceptive of hidden opportunities and interpersonal challenges. EQ can allow our emotions to become sources of useful information and even wisdom, as opposed to being distracting intrusions, and thereby can significantly increase our capacity for success. And it can help us be more resilient in the face of life pressures. For example, research has suggested that a higher EQ can help us to have less severe emotional reactions and to respond more constructively to the threat of possibly losing our jobs in the face of downsizing or corporate restructuring.[27]

Goleman's more recent book, written with Richard Boyatzis and Annie McKee, titled *Primal Leadership*, describes the important role of EQ for leadership effectiveness.[28] Specifically, based on decades of analysis in world class organizations, they argue that a leader's emotions are contagious. They call for leaders to resonate enthusiasm and energy in order to help their followers and organizations thrive. If leaders project negativity and dissonance, the authors predict their followers and organizations will flounder.

Steve Ballmer, CEO of perennially successful Microsoft, has sent a consistent message. In commenting on "the pillars of excellence" for business, he talks about the importance of emotionally charged factors such as excitement, courage, and optimism.[29] And when he talks about the need for vision in leadership, he points out its importance for getting people psyched up and enthused.

While EQ is clearly a very important concept to know about, its full benefit cannot be enjoyed unless we find meaningful ways of understanding its relevance to us personally and for applying it in our own lives. That is, being aware of what it is and that it is important are not enough. We need to find ways to increase our EQ on a continuing basis. This in turn can increase our overall capacity to cope with difficult feelings when they occur and to integrate the power and usefulness of healthy constructive feelings in our lives. Increasing our EQ needs to become a regular ongoing part of our daily experience.

The idea of lifelong learning has become a recognized reality of our complex and rapidly changing world. Continuing education at colleges, professional workshops, conferences, community education programs, online courses, and independent self-directed study are all part of our ongoing learning. All this is well and good and can keep us sharp now and growing even more for the challenges of tomorrow.

The problem, however, is when the dominant focus of these learning activities is restricted to concrete functional skill development in specific areas of work performance without consideration of emotional factors. For example, legendary money manager and investment expert Peter Lynch has emphasized the futility of studying only the mechanics of investing without recognizing the importance of emotions:

> The key to making money in stocks is not to get scared out of them. This point cannot be overemphasized. Every year finds a spate of books on how to pick stocks or find the winning mutual fund. But all this good information is useless without the willpower. In dieting and in stocks, it is the gut and not the head that determines the results. . . . The person who never bothers to think about the economy, blithely ignores the condition of the market, and invests on a regular schedule is better off than the person who studies and tries to time his investments, getting into stocks when he feels confident and out when he feels queasy.[30]

Whether in investing or countless other aspects of life, too often the emotional aspects of our personal effectiveness can be given short shrift in our ongoing personally chosen curriculum.

This presents us with yet another opportunity to make a disciplined choice. We can choose to seek out articles, books, workshops, courses, online offerings, or however else you feel motivated to learn, that specifically address increasing understanding and skill in dealing with emotions.

We can also observe and study our feelings. People spend years perfecting their golf game, tennis stroke, conditioning their bodies, or developing their professional knowledge in their technical field. Yet it is our feelings that ultimately wield power over the satisfaction we derive from any of these activities. We can have one of our best ever rounds of golf or turn in an outstanding performance on a project at work and still feel miserable. The miserable feeling may be due to a part of the process that we feel went poorly or because someone said something that upset us. We can increase our EQ by consciously studying our emotional responses to different situations. In the process we can learn more about how our emotions both put the joy into our life experiences as well as take it out. Sharpening our emotional intelligence deserves every bit as much priority, and arguably even more, than most aspects of our lives.

So an initial key to reaping the vast potential benefits of emotional discipline is to make the choice to enhance our EQ continuously by seeking out learning resources as well as studying our ongoing emotional experience. As we experience growth in this area and find ourselves gaining more power over how we feel, we will be naturally drawn to opportunities to further develop this distinctive aspect of our expertise. Newspaper and magazine articles will seem to jump out at us, and so will workshop and seminar announcements, web sites, and so forth. As we gain some sense of mastery and pride in our emotional awareness, knowledge, and skills, the foundation for our positive emotional discipline will be continuously reinforced. Choosing to increase our EQ is an essential part of emotional discipline and a key to increasing our power to choose how we feel.

Normally I would list helpful learning sources in the notes section or in an appendix. However, since this chapter is specifically focused on increasing your EQ through the learning choices you make, I will include a list of books you might consider studying to help increase your emotional intelligence. The following resources offer a good place to start building your EQ. You don't need to choose from only these books specifically, but I encourage you to consider working through one or more of them and to be on the lookout for other sources for increasing your EQ.

Some Suggested EQ Building Resources

In Chapter 1 I pointed out that the five key steps of an emotional discipline process incorporate some sound principles and strategies that have been addressed in detail in other books. The following books are suggested as additional reading both for help with specific aspects of the emotional discipline process as well as developing your overall EQ. They represent just a small sample of the many resources that you can choose to read, but they serve as a good starting place for study beyond this book.

Feeling Good: The New Mood Therapy by David D. Burns (New York: Avon Books, 1999) is a very thorough and helpful book for working with your thoughts that tend to correspond with your difficult feelings. It provides effective tools for analyzing and replacing dysfunctional beliefs and self-statements.

The Heart of the Soul: Emotional Awareness by Gary Zukav and Linda Francis (New York: Simon & Schuster, 2001) is a good resource for gaining more specific insights on becoming aware of your emotions. It addresses practical aspects of becoming more aware of and better understanding the physical sensations in the body that correspond with emotions as well as the thoughts that tend to accompany them.

Celebration of Discipline: The Path to Spiritual Growth by Richard J. Foster (San Francisco: HarperSanFrancisco, 1998) is a good reference for gaining understanding and guidance in applying "disciplines" as a means for growing spiritually, the primary historical usage of the term.

For a general treatment of the process of self-leadership, as a way to enhance your level of self-motivation and self-direction, and to increase your overall personal effectiveness, consider exploring the book I wrote with co-author Chris Neck: *Mastering Self-Leadership: Empowering Yourself for Personal Excellence,* (Upper Saddle River, NJ: Prentice Hall, 2nd edition, 1999, 3rd edition forthcoming in 2003).

Hooked on Feeling Bad: 3 Steps to Living a Life You Love! by Joyce Moskowitz (Davie, FL: Clear Vision Publishing,

2000) provides an interesting and straightforward way to examine your feelings and internal thoughts that can help reveal a deeper sense of how you see yourself at a core level.

Daniel Goleman's books *Emotional Intelligence: Why it Can Matter More Than IQ* and *Working with Emotional Intelligence* (New York: Bantam, 1995 and 1998 respectively) are very good sources for gaining a better understanding of the importance of your emotions and knowing how to intelligently live with and from them in your work and life. His newest book, co-authored with Richard Boyatzis and Annie McKee, *Primal Leadership: Realizing the Power of Emotional Intelligence* (Boston, Massachusetts: Harvard Business School Press, 2002) extends this work by examining the practical significance of EQ for leadership effectiveness.

Choice 5

Feel Your Feelings

~~~~~

The more you try to avoid suffering the more you suffer because smaller and more insignificant things begin to torture you in proportion to your fear of being hurt.

—Thomas Merton[31]

I must confess that the ideas in this chapter were the most difficult for me to work on. Why? Because the day I began to ponder them was September 11, 2001. I realize that 9/11 has been talked about and written about far and wide, and one more treatise about its place in history would not contribute much. Nevertheless, I believe it should be acknowledged, partly because of its vast impact on the emotional state of millions of people around the world, but perhaps even more so because of the dark challenge it poses regarding the idea that we can choose how we feel. What follows are some excerpts from what I originally wrote on 9/11.

~ ~ ~ ~ ~

As I sat down to begin work on these ideas I was confronted with a wave of difficult feelings to grapple with. Multiple U.S. planes had just been hijacked and turned into deadly weapons . . . on CNN I saw footage of an American jetliner crashing into one of the gigantic twin towers of the World Trade Center creating a huge explosion. The other tower had been hit in similar fashion just a few minutes earlier and was in flames. A little while later the huge twin towers, . . . housing thousands of civilian workers and visitors, both collapsed.

Over the next few minutes more devastating reports . . . an explosion at the Pentagon . . . Another plane crash in Pennsylvania . . . Evacuations of the White House, the Capitol, the Treasury, and then all federal buildings in Washington D.C. . . . and major airports across the country.

I sat stunned. I felt as though I had just sustained a series of powerful emotional blows. Could such a cruel act be put in perspective? . . . and I was faced with the irony that I was engaged in writing a book that argues that the way we feel is a choice. This is indeed a difficult claim when external tragic events send our feelings into a turbulent frenzy. Even in the small college town of Amherst, Massachusetts, a seeming haven from big city tragedies, the headline of our local newspaper read "Tears and Prayers" and talked of "the most devastating terrorist onslaught ever waged against the United States" and of "digging out the dead."

~ ~ ~ ~ ~

Thinking about emotional discipline with this kind of overpowering backdrop challenged me to the core. What could I suggest about feelings that might be of help to myself and others? Indeed, some situations are so extreme that it may appear that the best choice we can make is to just hang on and live through them, overwhelming feelings and all. (I address this idea in greater detail in Chapter 7 when I talk about "weathering emotional storms.")

Nevertheless, I concluded, we recognize many situations (difficult meetings, setbacks at work, arguments) that we should be able to deal with more effectively, but we often find ourselves responding to them with a deep loss of composure or by avoiding them altogether. For many of life's emotionally challenging situations there is much value in learning to squarely face them and to feel the feelings they provoke. My thoughts went to more spiritually oriented literature. I thought of writers who advocate inner reflection and meditation such as Jon Kabat-Zinn, author of the best-seller *Wherever You Go, There You Are,* who teach that when we meditate we can just sit with whatever comes up, even difficult feelings.[32] We can simply be with our thoughts and emotions nonjudgmentally and without any sense that we have to change them.

This suggests a powerful way to deal with difficult feelings and to begin to transform them. Don't retreat. Instead go in closer and be with the inner struggle. Try to trace it to its source. For example, try picturing the feelings as though they were a person, only fuzzier and less defined, whom you are not getting along with, perhaps someone you consider to be a direct adversary or antagonist. Recognize that you could try to avoid this individual and find yourself constantly worrying that you might have a chance encounter. And you might try to slip into the shadows if you ever spot this person heading your way. This approach would produce continuous uneasiness and discomfort.

Another approach is to walk up and look this person straight in the eye, and invite a dialogue on how to repair the relationship. Similarly, you can move in close, go right into your difficult feelings, and allow a process of getting to know and understand them better. Metaphorically, you can look your feelings right in the eye and ask "what are you?" or "who are you?" and courageously stay right there with them. And when you realize that they can't really harm you (their only weapon is what you allow to happen in your mind) and that you have the strength to face them, you can ask yourself what all the fuss is about. This may be a scary thing to do at first, but stay with it if you can. Allow your feelings to be just as they are but also try to understand them better and to learn from them. The focus on learning can replace much of the fearful energy with curiosity and a desire to make healthy changes.

Of course, if you find facing your feelings too difficult and more than you can bear, you may want to seek the help of a professional counselor. Usually, though, you will find that even the most difficult feelings are bearable, and that realization alone will increase your inner strength. Sometimes you will even discover that at the heart of difficult feelings there are really nothing but passing thoughts, a kind of wispy mental fog that when faced squarely simply dissipates.

While writing this book I tried this very approach on several occasions, especially during disagreements with others in my work or personal life. Even if they criticized me directly, I was better able to remain relatively calm and effective. I simply tried to recognize my growing feelings and confront them rather than the other person. I tried to understand my feelings and where they were coming from. Interestingly, not only did my difficult feelings seem to disappear in many cases, but the other person seemed to respond to my steady and calm response and became much more cooperative.

The next time you have difficult feelings and find yourself wanting to escape the inner discomfort, I encourage you to resist the impulse. Instead move in closer, study, and learn. Feel your feelings. In making this choice I can almost guarantee that you will feel and be a lot better soon.

Choice 6

Emotional Kung Fu

~~~~~

The greatest martial arts are the gentlest.
They allow the attacker the opportunity to fall down.
The greatest generals do not rush into every battle.
They offer the enemy many opportunities
to make self-defeating errors.

—Lao Tzu[33]

n kung fu, an ancient Chinese art of self-defense, emphasis is placed on using any attacking force to your advantage. Instead of resisting a direct assault, the practitioner
averts and redirects the energy. For example, if a punch is
thrown at chest level, the defender might fluidly turn 90
degrees to avert the blow while adding an additional push
or pull "helping" the attacker to proceed in the direction
he or she was already heading. Instead of pitting strength
against strength, kung fu calls for using any force thrown
your way to actually help you accomplish an outcome that
you desire, such as sending opponents to the ground with
the energy of their attack.

As pointed out by the 2,500 year old writings in the
Tao Te Ching (known as the Tao), credited to the ancient
Chinese philosopher Lao Tzu: "The person who initiates
the attack is off center and easily thrown." However, it also
goes on to say, "Even so, have respect for an attacker. Never
surrender your compassion or use your skill to harm another needlessly."[34] The same logic can be applied to emotional conflicts. Rather than resisting an emotional attack,
we can use its energy to work toward a solution.

This strategy can be very useful when we are confronted with interpersonal conflicts. In the book *Getting to
Yes* authors Roger Fisher and William Ury prescribe just
this approach.[35] They point out that in emotionally
charged conflicts, people will often do three things: force-
fully state their position, attack our ideas, and attack us.
They advise that in facing such an assault we should resist
the temptation to push back, defend ourselves, or reject
their ideas. Instead we can sidestep and deflect the force of

the attack to use their strength to serve our (and their) ends. Specifically, they prescribe inviting criticism and advice that could reveal a solution, recasting the attack as an attack on the problem rather than you, and asking questions rather than making statements.

For example, imagine the following exchange between two co-workers who work in the same department.

~ ~ ~ ~ ~

"Lisa, I can't believe the changes you proposed for the way we report our travel expenses! The process is already screwed up enough without adding mindless details that will make it even more time consuming!"

"I'm glad we both agree, Sarah, that the current procedure is very ineffective. What is it that you don't like about the changes I have proposed?"

"Well that's right, Lisa, I do think changes need to be made, but your proposal adds still another form. I think if I have to fill out one more form around here I'm going to scream!"

"I see. So your primary concern is that we not add yet another form to all the red tape that we have to wade through around here. You have a good point. Do you see a way that we might be able to change the process without adding another form?"

"Well I must admit I hate the old form—it is very poorly organized and it asks for a lot of unnecessary detail. If I had my way we would just throw it out."

"Interesting idea but it does seem that there are some parts of the original form that are required by corporate policy. . . ."

*"Why can't we just add those few items to your new pro-
posed form at the very top?" Sarah interrupted now in a bit
less exasperated tone.*

*"Good idea, Sarah. I don't see why we couldn't do that as
long as we make sure items 1 through 6 and 9 and 11 are included," Lisa responded, while studying the two forms on her
desk. "I was not pleased with the idea of adding another form to
the process either, but the old form is so confusing and tedious."*

*"I agree," said Sarah, now sounding pleased. "Imagine if
we could finally get rid of that old form. And now that I look
at the way you've laid out your new one, it does fit our department's needs much better. I'd be glad to back you up with this
idea at the next department meeting."*

*"That would be great, Sarah. I think the solution we've
formulated together could really help us all out. We seem to
make a good team."*

*"I'll tell you what, Lisa. If you give me another copy of the
two forms (she had thrown them away in disgust when she first
received them attached to a copy of Lisa's proposal), I'll work
on developing a combined prototype that we can present."*

"Thanks, Sarah. That would be great!"

~ ~ ~ ~ ~

This same kind of approach can be used for internal emotional conflicts. For example, rather than fighting your
feelings you can acknowledge the importance you place on
whatever it is that's bothering you. You can also use the energy of the emotion to place more focus on the problem
and ask yourself how you might be able to improve the situation. The key is to avoid fighting the strength of the

emotion directly but rather redirecting its strength to work toward a desired end.

Emotional kung fu can be an effective self-defense process for your life. With practice, much of the seemingly negative emotion that comes your way, from both outside and within, can become an important energy supply for positive change. Choosing to use this energy to your advantage, rather than fighting it, can be a key part of practicing emotional discipline to feel and be better in your work and life.

Choice 7

Weather Emotional Storms

~ ~ ~ ~ ~ ~

Men suffer from thinking more than anything else.

—Leo Tolstoy

Never make a permanent decision based on a temporary storm. No matter how raging the billows are today, remind yourself: "This too shall pass!"

—T. D. Jakes

I don't know about you, but I've never known anyone who does not experience low moods some of the time. When we are in a down mood, our whole experience of life can suffer. At such times, the same things that might otherwise leave us relatively unaffected can seem much more significant and discouraging. We can even get caught in a downward spiral in which we feed the mood with additional discouraging thoughts, exaggerating the negative and ignoring the positive. And sometimes these mood cycles can seem almost overwhelming.

I like to think of these internal emotional swings as being analogous to the weather. Just like the weather, sometimes we have internal storms. These emotional storms might be triggered by a series of disappointing events. Or they might be affected by hormonal swings, some junk food we ate, or by a lack of sleep. All kinds of factors can help trigger our inner turbulent weather, but a leading cause, as well as a potential remedy, is in the way we are thinking at the time. More specifically, it is important to recognize what is going on and to put things in perspective. "OK, I'm experiencing a difficult mood, so what? There is no need to make it a bigger deal than it is. I can choose to do something that will help lift the mood—perhaps go for a walk, take a relaxation break, watch a funny movie—or I can just wait it out. It will pass."

Of course, this logic is not meant to address more serious health issues, such as clinical depression, that require professional help. But more often than not, by choosing to think about our mood differently, and choosing constructive action if it is available, we can improve how we feel. Even if an action remedy does not seem possible at the moment, we can simply choose to "weather the storm." Either way we have a choice. And this is a powerful emotional discipline strategy. Instead of fighting the powerful inner gale, simply let it run its course. Instead of fighting against the wind, simply glide with it and even harness it for your advantage.

I encourage you to consider the following poetic image of these ideas. As you do, think about the times when you have felt discouraged and see if you can identify with the storyteller's voice. You might even try reading this when you find that an inner storm has moved into your consciousness and mood state. If you are not a fan of poetry, you may choose to skip over this poem as well as the small amount of poetry contained later in the book. After all, a major message of this book is that you have the power to choose. But before making this choice, I hope you will consider a statement made by best-selling author Martin Rutte about the usefulness of poetry when it is brought to business managers in particular: "Managers . . . begin to realize other aspects of themselves. Poetry helps them delve more deeply into their creative selves, it rounds them out and it helps contribute to new insights, both personal and corporate."[36]

The Eagle in the Sparrow
I look down and see the shadow of a sad, weak sparrow,
always straining against the wind,
and as the swirling sand bites its flesh
it struggles with all its might to find its wings
bent sharp against its weary burdened back.
I see this, my shadow, warped and twisted on the earth
and sorrow burns deep scars on my darkened hope within.

I have seen the glass and it is not that it is half empty
that brings such despair.
Instead, it is that the part that is poured out
is the nectar for which I long and need.
I cry within.
I do stop and the rose I do smell but it is the wrong rose
>*for sure.*
I do have a soul and a spirit but they have long forgotten
and know each other not.
As I squeeze my last blood red drop of courage
into the urgent flap of my wings
I am surely lost on the very course I have charted.
I am lost exactly where I have chosen to be.
Every landmark I plotted is here
and I am more lost than I am alive.
In this dark knowing I finally find my hope
in the pure truth that I have none at all.
I will never reach my destined place on this course
no matter the strain, the blood, the tears,
the ripping of my soul,
as my wings are torn from the sad creature I have made
>*myself.*
And in this hopeless hope,
formed of ironic cleansing disdain,
I discover the wind.
Not just the wind but the wind within the wind.
I stop flapping, let go, and begin to float
shifting in the cool soft air of my life,
my true life yet unforged.
Everything is new and I glide, then soar,
effortlessly toward the heavens.

My wings embrace the sky and at last
my soul again knows my spirit.
The nectar is not in the glass
because it has already filled my heart
and the smelled rose is at once every rose.
I don't struggle and strain because now I live.
The sand and the wind share my ride,
brothers and sisters at my side,
stroking and embracing me.
I watch the whole world breathe pure beauty in and out.
My heavy weight evaporates with my sigh
and fills the clouds that stroke my hair.
I look down.
The sad sparrow shadow is no more.
I see only the large outstretched wings of an eagle
on the wind of all winds
for which it always belonged.

—Charles C. Manz

Perhaps we sometimes try too hard to fight our problems. There are times when struggling with the forces that seem to be against us is not wise and even self-defeating. Sometimes, the best choice for feeling better in life is to simply weather the storms, and perhaps relax with them as we ride their winds, and wait for the sun to come out again in our emotional universe. And while you wait, remember the words of 19th century philosopher Friedrich Nietzsche,

"One must have chaos within to give birth to a dancing star."

Our mind is the foundation for the way we feel. Our experience of life originates in our thinking. When we feel bad, more often than not, we are thinking about our immediate circumstances in suboptimal ways. As we learn and choose to think in new and healthier ways, the way we feel tends to be naturally and positively enhanced.

~~~~~~~~~~~

Part Two

Mind

~~~~~

*The Mind is its own place, and in itself can make
a Heaven of Hell, a Hell of Heaven.*

—John Milton

Choice 8

Happiness Is a Choice

~~~~~

Happiness is as a butterfly which, when pursued,
is always beyond our grasp, but which,
if you will sit down quietly, may alight upon you.

—Nathaniel Hawthorne

If only we'd stop trying to be happy,
we could have a pretty good time.
— Edith Wharton[37]

For many, happiness is the ultimate treasure sought in the quest for a full and satisfying life. Yet, as the above quotes suggest, our pursuit of happiness may be the primary obstacle to ever really experiencing it. This is indeed an odd and challenging characteristic of happiness.

In his book *You Can Be Happy No Matter What*, bestselling author Richard Carlson insightfully discusses this challenge:

> Happiness is a state of mind, not a set of circumstances. . . you can never find happiness by "searching," because the moment you do, you imply it is found outside yourself. Happiness isn't outside yourself. It is a feeling—the natural feeling of your innate healthy psychological functioning. . . . When you understand that happiness is nothing more than a feeling, you can help it grow and maintain itself when you do feel it. . . . Happiness requires no effort at all. In fact, it's more of a letting go of unhappiness than it is a striving for happiness."[38]

That happiness can be viewed as a feeling originating inside of ourselves is perhaps not too surprising to most of us. However, the idea that it's the pursuit of happiness that can actually keep us from having it is more challenging to grasp. After all, isn't the pursuit of happiness one of the fundamental rights that the founding fathers of the United States tried to build into the very fabric of the nation? If pursuing happiness is not the way to become happy, then what is? According to Carlson the key to experiencing happiness may rest in letting go of unhappiness.

And he is in good company when he suggests this powerfully different perspective. The Dalai Lama offers a similar message. His view is that we are often primary contributors to the pain and suffering in our lives that can keep us from the happiness we desire:

> . . . there are many ways in which we actively contribute to our own experience of mental unrest and suffering. Although, in general, mental and emotional afflictions themselves can come naturally, often it is our own reinforcement of those negative emotions that makes them so much worse.

To elaborate on this important idea, he goes on to explain that a primary way we add to the pain and suffering that causes us so much unhappiness is by:

> being overly sensitive, overreacting to minor things, and sometimes taking things too personally. We tend to take small things too seriously and blow them out of proportion, while at the same time we often remain indifferent to the really important things, those things which have profound effects on our lives and long-term consequences and implications."[39]

Happiness is a choice. This is a powerful and hopeful idea. But the truth of this statement does not rest in the pursuit of wishes and desires outside ourselves. The key is not to chase after those things in the world that cause a sense of elation, a temporary high. Such moments can be pleasurable, but they do not offer real lasting happiness. Rather, they offer little more than a momentary emotional lift. To count on such moments for our happiness in life is undependable at best. At worst, we are left at the mercy of external events, approval of others, and momentary and continuously shifting emotional states. The real key, suggested by the Dalai Lama, Richard Carlson, and likely your own life experience if you listen to what it has to say, is to let go of unhappiness.

Consider the following story about Ramone, who has just met Kyle during an exercise at a personal development seminar offered in their city.

~ ~ ~ ~ ~

Participants were asked to find a partner to talk about how they felt about their current quality of life. This was designed to prepare them for some personal goal setting. Kyle described his life to Ramone in a surprisingly candid manner. He welcomed the opportunity to get some things off his chest with someone he was not likely to see again. Kyle seemed to "have it all" and yet he seemed very unhappy. He talked about his many disappointments right up to their next break.

During the break Ramone took a short walk by himself to stretch his legs while he pondered his own satisfaction with life relative to Kyle's. Ramone noted that Kyle grew up in a privileged upper-class family with two attentive parents and a supportive sister. He had received much encouragement throughout his school years and had received several scholastic honors, eventually earning an Ivy League college degree. And in Kyle's words he had "married well" and was moving into the beginnings of a successful career as an executive. Kyle admitted that he pretty much had it all, yet he felt surprisingly dissatisfied. He could easily name a long list of disappointments and frustrations in his life. For Kyle, it seemed that the glass was well over half full in his life, but all he seemed to focus on was the part of the glass that was empty.

Ramone puzzled at this. He had to admit that he generally felt pretty good about his life, despite a difficult background and a current modest lifestyle. He came from a poor household, and his father left his family when he was a small child. Being single with two children, Ramone's mother often had to work two jobs at a time to pay the bills. Ramone and his sister experienced a variety of childcare arrangements while growing up in a low-income part of town. And many of the adults he encountered, in and outside of school, were very harsh and punitive.

As Ramone grew into his adult years, he was initially bitter about his childhood. His mother had rarely been around, and when she was she was usually cranky. And he received little encouragement from his overworked teachers in the crowded classes he attended. Eventually, despite this difficult background, Ramone managed to get a part-time job and pay his way through a local community college for two years and then through the state university to receive his BA degree. Now, a few years later, he is married and has a full-time office job with modest pay and benefits. His income and his wife's combined barely cover their monthly bills. Yet they have been discussing starting a family and the possibility of purchasing a home within a year or so. Ramone likes the idea but cannot currently see how they can make this work given their tight finances.

Overall, Ramone works hard and struggles to make ends meet but is very content with his life. He reflects back from time to time on his difficult past, but more often he focuses on being thankful for all he has and the positive possibilities for his future. Somewhere along the way Ramone made a choice to let go of the unhappiness of his past. Now he enjoys a stable kind of contentment in his life that seems to transcend his circumstances.

~ ~ ~ ~ ~

Admittedly, the story of Ramone and Kyle is a bit simplistic, but it does raise an important feature of life. The real life stories of those who seem to have the most, the lives of the rich and famous, are often very sad. Divorce, drug and alcohol abuse, painful psychiatric problems, and a variety of other telltale signs of unhappiness litter the landscape of many of what would seem should be enviable lives.

In the end, the idea that happiness is a choice is quite compelling. More than riches, fame, and good fortune, a decision to be happy seems to be the key. Yet making this choice is tricky. The key lesson is that happiness is not something that can be effectively sought directly. Rather, it is the choice to let go of unhappiness that provides the surest bridge to meaningful long-term happiness.

Choice 9

Meditate for a Better Life

~~~~~

*All of humanity's problems stem from man's inability to
sit quietly in a room alone.*

—Blaise Pascal

*S*he entered her office, quietly closed the door, and sat in a comfortable straight-backed chair. She knew this was a time in the work day that she would not likely be disturbed. And she had let her colleagues know that when her door was closed, unless it was an emergency, she appreciated their waiting until later to contact her.

She closed her eyes and began to focus on her own deep breathing. Each breath was taken in through her nose and into the abdomen and exhaled through her slightly parted lips. Her belly expanded and retracted with each breath, but her chest moved very little. She gradually relaxed more deeply with no effort beyond focusing on each breath. If her mind wandered, she gently returned her attention to her breathing. Fifteen minutes later a preset alarm clock made the sound of ocean waves and she gradually opened her eyes. Feeling refreshed she slowly rose to her feet and opened her door, now feeling ready to face the rest of the day.

~ ~ ~ ~ ~

This scenario describes one of the simplest and most effective meditation techniques. Meditation requires no special equipment and can be done almost anywhere. For many types of meditation it is preferable that you have access to a quiet, private, comfortable location and a place to sit upright for a few minutes. However, other forms of meditation can be practiced in various postures from standing to lying down and even in public settings.

One of the most effective foundations for meditation centers on a concept known as "mindfulness." Best-selling author and the founder of the Stress Reduction Clinic at the University of Massachusetts, Jon Kabat-Zinn (also mentioned in Chapter 5) has described it like this: "Mindfulness means paying attention in a particular way: on purpose, in the present moment, and nonjudgmentally."[40] He explains that this can increase our awareness and clarity, help us get unstuck to be in better touch with our wisdom and vitality, and help us enhance the direction and quality of our lives. The mindfulness meditation training offered at his clinic has not only enriched the lives of many hundreds of people but provided dramatic health benefits for even severely ill patients.

I personally have been practicing meditation for several years and have found it to help me be more focused, reduce my level of stress, and substantially improve my overall sense of well-being. I meditate for about 20 minutes almost every morning and have found this daily investment to provide benefits worth many times the short period I devote to the practice. If my schedule is very tight on a given day, I still meditate, even if only for a couple minutes while sitting in a waiting room before an appointment.

I have learned and tried many forms of meditation. One approach was described at the outset of this chapter. Here I will share a couple other meditation approaches designed for a more conventional sitting posture in a private location, but many books and audiotapes are available to help guide you through a vast array of alternatives.

~ ~ ~ ~ ~

He sat on a small cushion on the carpet of his bedroom floor. He had already taken the phone off the hook to make sure he would not be disturbed. His back was comfortably straight, and he breathed deeply in and out of his abdomen. He closed his eyes and mentally pictured himself in the middle of a beautiful rain forest. If he found his mind wondering, he simply observed his thoughts, not attaching significance beyond watching them pass through his consciousness. He viewed each thought as though it were a bird or plant or some other element in the forest. Any sounds that came into the room, or physical feelings he experienced, such as from the contact of his body with the cushion or floor, were also pictured as originating from the rain forest. He relaxed deeper and deeper, mentally becoming absorbed by his imagined environment.

~ ~ ~ ~ ~

Mental imagery can serve as a powerful aid to meditation. Picturing peaceful settings that trigger deep relaxing physical responses can produce profound health effects. But meditation can be much more basic. One of the earliest approaches centers on the simple repetition of a mantra such as the word "om" or "one." Generally it is advisable to select a word that does not evoke emotion but instead is neutral to you. By effortlessly focusing on repeating a mantra for several minutes (usually quietly in the mind), very beneficial states of healing relaxation can be achieved.

For those who prefer a more spiritual approach, many forms of prayer can serve as a powerful form of meditation.

By spending a few minutes quietly focused on God (or however you understand a healthy higher spiritual power), repeating uplifting centering-focused prayers, or even imagining yourself flowing into and connecting with the "oneness" of the universe, beneficial states of mind and body are possible.

Well-known author Richard Carlson (mentioned in the previous chapter) has pointed out that "meditation teaches you to be calm by giving you the experience of absolute relaxation. It teaches you to be at peace."[41] My own experience has been that on some days it does just that. On other days, however, when my mind is more active and perhaps I'm more agitated, meditation still helps me to be more centered and less reactive to difficulties I face, even if I don't enjoy as much relaxation and peace. It has become a central part of a personal lifestyle choice that enables me to feel and be better.

I can't recommend it enough. Meditation can help train you to live more healthily with your thoughts and emotions, which can establish an improved capacity to keep things in perspective and to not become overwhelmed by frustrating circumstances. And the effects of meditation are cumulative. It is not a quick fix, but it can introduce much of value into your life over time, when practiced consistently. It can help create a calm center in your life to draw upon when you need it. Consequently, you are less likely to be prone to take situations personally, fly off the handle, respond to others dysfunctionally, or have any number of other unfortunate reactions to emotionally charged situations. If you are not already doing so on a regular basis, I encourage you to make the emotional discipline choice to meditate for a better life.

Choice 10

Mental Reframing

~~~~~

We don't see things as they are, we see them as we are.

—Anais Nin[42]

I n my previous book, *The Power of Failure,* I wrote about many themes that challenge typical modes of thinking:

> To succeed more, fail more. Sometimes when you win you lose. Sometimes when you lose you win. Look for opportunities in obstacles. See the magnificent in the minimal. Sometimes get in over your head to get ahead. To be truly successful you must learn how to fail successfully.

The book addresses a variety of ways that life setbacks can be turned into opportunities for success. Many of the strategies I describe involve rethinking difficult circumstances. Examples are wide ranging. They include the classic story about how a failed attempt to create a new kind of glue resulted in the invention of Post-it notes at 3M, investment strategies that purposely target as buying opportunities securities in markets that are dropping sharply, and Bill Gates's view that many of Microsoft's most successful products resulted from previous product failures.

In fact, many of the greatest achievements in the history of the world resulted from repeated failures that were treated as opportunities to learn and stepping-stones to success. The invention of the airplane that enabled humans to fly, revolutionary drugs that cured deadly illnesses, and the invention of the light bulb that brought light into the darkness are just a few of these seeming miracles (at the time) achieved in the wake of repeated failures.

In the latter example, Thomas Edison made hundreds of unsuccessful attempts before finally inventing a light bulb that worked. At one point in this long and challenging process, he was asked how he could continue this pursuit after failing more than a thousand times. He reportedly replied that he had not failed. Rather, he had succeeded in discovering a thousand ways that didn't work. This powerful reframing of events helped establish the motivation to go on. It fostered a mental attitude needed for turning what could have been feelings of hopelessness into a sense of progress and hopefulness.

Bill Gates has offered powerful advice for applying this kind of thinking to a practical everyday business example—how to address unhappy customers.[43] He suggests that customer complaints should be integrated into the development of products and services. Somewhat surprisingly, he prescribes a focus on the most unhappy customers of all. Instead of avoiding these, perhaps rather extreme, critics of what the organization has to offer, he points out that they offer a rich source of information and a great opportunity.

By finding out about their unhappy experiences and what they would like, useful insights can be obtained. This knowledge can then be passed on to employees who are in the best position to use it in developing and improving products and services. Gates points out that this approach allows discouraging bad news to be turned into an exhilarating improvement process. As a result, the most difficult customers, who seem to represent the biggest obstacles, become the greatest opportunity for future success.

This example illustrates in a practical way the idea of mental reframing. Almost any situation, no matter how seemingly bleak or negative, can be reframed in a more constructive and positive way. A significant mistake is an opportunity to learn what not to do in the future, and perhaps provides insight about a new and better approach. A lost job offers an opportunity for a new exciting career. An argument provides a chance to learn something about relationships and how people differ in the way they see things. A stressful event is an occasion to become stronger and more confident about being able to withstand challenges. And so on.

The important lesson is that every challenge in life can be viewed from different angles. Even the most difficult situations almost always offer some advantage or opportunity. The key is to use flexible thinking with a good dose of optimism. With practice, a choice to use mental reframing can become an important emotional discipline tool for enhancing the way you feel about and experience life.

Choice 11

Direct Your Inner Theater

~~~~~

All the world's a stage, And all the men and women merely players. They have their exits and their entrances, And one man in his time plays many parts.

—William Shakespeare, *As You Like It* (II, vii)

One of the most effective emotional discipline choices we can make calls us to apply the power of the theater. I'm not talking about Broadway plays or going to the movies. Rather, I'm talking about the elaborate, moving productions that perform in our minds every day.

Neuro-Linguistic Programming (NLP), developed in the early 1970s by Richard Bandler and John Grinder, offers tools for capturing the power of our inner theaters. It focuses on the content of our subjective experiences and offers a practical approach for addressing how we think. NLP "holds that people act based on internal representations of the world and not the world itself."[44] Many different popular self-help writers and trainers have used NLP as part of their message. Perhaps the best known of these NLP advocates is the popular Guru Anthony Robbins.

Robbins and other NLP enthusiasts prescribe a number of mental exercises and techniques for mastering the power of our mental representations of the world—our inner theaters. Here I will share examples of some of the more basic strategies that I personally have found to be especially powerful.[45]

One strategy is to creatively and playfully alter the nature of internal images and self-talk. For example, imagine that you find yourself using demoralizing negative self-talk after making a mistake. By changing your inner voice and its location, you can reduce or eliminate the destructive effects. Let's say that you heard a harsh version of your own voice at the top of your head saying, "What a stupid thing to do. I really screwed up this time. I can't do anything right." Rather than allowing this self-abuse to run unchecked, you can make a choice to hear the voice of Donald Duck, Mickey Mouse, or Barney the Dinosaur coming from the little toe on your left foot. You can choose countless other nonthreatening, entertaining, and funny voices as well as creatively absurd locations. Experiment and discover what combinations seem to work for you. Making the choice to create this very different kind of mental representation can change an internal destructive process into a more pleasant, even humorous and entertaining, one.

As another strategy, the same kind of approach can be used when relating to others. Imagine an annoying coworker is delivering harsh words (and probably for something you didn't even do). "What a surprise . . . you screwed up again. You're lucky that there are some competent people around here to clean up after your incompetence." Now see him shrink down to a one-foot tall miniature version of himself with a huge pot belly and watch his nose and ears grow to 10 times their normal size. Picture him in a ballerina suit with a big floppy polka dot clown hat. And imagine he has the voice of your favorite cartoon character (one person recently told me her favorite voice to impose on an obnoxious critic is Popeye's lady friend Olive Oyl). Such mental choices can change a bothersome annoying situation into at least a benign one, and potentially even a comedic and entertaining experience.

Other strategies can be used to alter our mental images or pictures. Think of an event in your past that was moderately (don't start with your most extreme painful memory at this stage) upsetting to you. Try to imagine yourself back in the situation and the difficult feelings it produces. Now run the same scene through your mind again, only this time imagine that you are seeing it projected onto a movie screen and that you are watching it from a comfortable seat in an auditorium, perhaps with a tub of popcorn in your lap and your favorite drink at your side. Seeing yourself as an observer rather than actually being in the scene will likely significantly reduce its emotional impact. You can even visualize the movie you are watching as changing to a faded black and white image that is becoming smaller and moving farther away from you. Once again the difficult feelings attached to the experience should be reduced.

You can also use a similar strategy in the current moment when you encounter difficult experiences. For example, if your boss or a co-worker is venting his or her frustration at you and you find your stress level is quickly rising, try dissociating from the experience in your mind. Mentally imagine that you are watching the scene from a position above or off to the side. Essentially, shift your awareness out of your body so that you become an observer rather than a direct participant. You can even picture yourself safely behind a transparent barrier made of bulletproof glass if you like. It takes practice, but as you train your mind to dissociate from painful memories or ongoing experiences, you can take much of the sting out of difficult circumstances. The idea is not to avoid your responsibilities or lose touch with reality but rather to make a conscious choice to mentally process situations in a way that helps you to introduce some healthy emotional discipline and to improve your personal effectiveness.

All the world is a stage indeed, especially the one inside your head. You can choose to change the scenery, colors, costumes, voices, appearances of the actors, and any other details that you like. You can even change the point of view of the unfolding story from that of direct participant to a dissociated observer. It can be your own empowering choice to make if you learn the emotional discipline strategy of becoming the director of your inner mental theater.

Choice 12

Think and Grow Richly Alive

~ ~ ~ ~ ~

Thinking is the hardest work there is,
which is the probable reason why so few engage in it.

—Henry Ford, Sr.[46]

The significant problems that we face
cannot be solved at the same level of thinking
we were at when we created them.

—Albert Einstein

T hought is arguably the most powerful activity we can do in our lives. Unfortunately, it is easy to fall into the trap of allowing our minds to run out of control with shallow thoughts and avoid more meaningful thinking. Of course, at a minimum we think all the time in habitual and surface level ways that enable us to survive. But do we think in ways that help us to learn, grow, and develop into our fuller potential? Do we choose and nurture meaningful thinking, or do we allow our thoughts to occur almost randomly in ways that frequently disrupt our lives rather than enrich them? To borrow from the title of the classic best-seller *Think and Grow Rich*, do we think in ways that help us to grow richly alive?

In this chapter I want to share one of the most powerful secrets to effective thinking that I have ever discovered. It is what I call 3rd level thinking. Let me start with the analogy of the different "persons" that can be used when writing a story. We say we are writing in 1st, 2nd, or 3rd person depending on whether we tell the story by focusing on our own experience, addressing the reader directly, or describing the experience of others.

Similarly, your thoughts can be viewed as occurring at three levels. The difference in this case, however, is that 1st, 2nd, and 3rd level thinking all take place within your own mind.

The 1st level consists of thoughts that enter, or perhaps more accurately invade, your mind in response to immediate events, or even out of the blue. This is the most basic thinking level, sometimes containing thoughts that trigger emotions and that can be very arousing. You might suddenly think about how a colleague publicly criticized you in a recent meeting, even though the event occurred two days ago and has no apparent connection with what you are doing right now. This level of thinking not only begins to trigger emotional and physiological reactions, such as those that accompany frustration or anger, but it triggers the 2nd level of thinking.

At the 2nd level you think about your 1st level thoughts. For example, you might think "that lousy SOB, how dare he criticize me publicly. After all the ways I have helped him over the years and all the mistakes he has made in the past." And who is suffering from the resulting indignant emotional reaction? It's only you. The person who delivered the insult, and doesn't even know about this internal conversation, is unaffected.

Often, this is as far as the thinking goes. You are left fuming about the unfair criticism. In other cases it might be the mistake the waiter made on your bill or the way you messed up during a recent presentation. Or it could be the poor service received from a vendor you have supported for years, or the dissatisfaction you feel with your lot in life that seems so unfair given how hard you have worked and how noble you have been. This pattern of 1st and 2nd level thinking can leave you feeling upset, dissatisfied, and in a generally lousy mood. Unless . . .

This is where 3rd level thinking comes in. You can choose to disengage from your current thinking process and observe what is going on, as though you are watching two people interact. You can stop and reflect on the 1st and 2nd level thinking. Normally this will occur as mostly relatively detached nonverbal observation of your thoughts. But if it were put into words, it might sound something like this, "I see that a thought about the past criticism invaded my mind and then I've been caught up in internal dialogue reacting to my thought. And I've been getting very upset about some thoughts in my head that I didn't even invite in there . . . very interesting."

This new level of thinking can almost immediately free you from the cycle of negativity and uncomfortable emotion. By choosing to focus on this 3rd level, you are lifted above the upsetting internal chatter. By choosing 3rd level thinking you are freed to appreciate the moment and to regain some sense of balance in your life. Instead of experiencing life through these upsetting thoughts, they simply become another aspect of life to observe. Instead of allowing your thoughts to essentially push you around on the inside, you are able to be relatively unaffected by them because you can see them for what they are—temporary invaders of your mental world that have power only to the extent you give it to them.

To further reinforce these ideas, from a different more artistic perspective, consider the following poem.

Thoughtful Invasion

Fleeting thoughts, haunting thoughts,
rising, turning, leaping, fuming, always intruding.
They come, they go, they hold the mind and heart.

In themselves their significance limited but power great,
shaking the very soul of my soul I am sent tumbling.

But it is my thinking about my thoughts,
not just the thoughts, that wounds or heals.

I royalize my thoughts . . . enshrine, empower, immortalize.
Yet they are but fleeting, leaping, invading, uninvited self-
important guests.

So I am left with the challenge, the journey, the inner quest.
It is my thinking about my thinking about my thoughts that
holds the promise.
This alone can allow a letting go to live and to be.
And in this thinking my mental chains can be returned to the
electric dust from which they sprung.
Come fleeting thoughts, come haunting invading thoughts,
for I am set free.

—Charles C. Manz

The concept of 3rd level thinking also applies to what appears to be positive, even euphoric, thinking. It's true that the thoughts that invade your mind can be of upbeat ideas that trigger exciting 2nd level thinking and emotions. These "positive" thoughts can also be overly stimulating and actually produce stress.

For example, you might think of a promising new project idea or a potential lucrative investment. Next, you begin to fantasize about all the fame and wealth that it could bring you. Soon you find yourself fixated on this possibility and so excited that you even have difficulty sleeping at night. You may also be so captivated by the possibilities that you don't bother to research the facts surrounding this potential opportunity. As a result you find yourself at best left with a temporary surge of excited energy. At worst, you are confronted with an uninformed reckless risk of your time and resources, and your exaggerated feelings may cause you to move ahead with costly results.

Of course, much of the time it is just fine to let this process of positive thought and emotion unfold naturally, as long as it doesn't lead to taking reckless risks or costing too much sleep. But as the old saying goes, what goes up must come down. Eventually, these positive thoughts and feelings will fade or even abruptly give way to the reality of the challenges of the moment and other less positive thoughts. All this means that being able to use 3rd level thinking, even on your positive upbeat thoughts, can help you to be freed from the powerful grip of the reactionary tides of whirling feelings.

It takes some work to establish an ongoing ability to see things from the 3rd level. It may seem a bit confusing at first, but the key is to choose to think at a different level. That is, you need to purposely think about your thinking about your thoughts. This choice can put you in touch with where your real power lies to become richly alive and is especially important when you find yourself reacting dysfunctionally to uninvited invading thoughts.

Choice 13

The Manifesting Power of Positive Thinking

~~~~~

There are only two ways to live your life. One is as though nothing is a miracle. The other is as though everything is a miracle.

—Albert Einstein

Some men see things as they are and ask why. I dream things that never were and say, why not?

—George Bernard Shaw

Norman Vincent Peale's book *The Power of Positive Thinking* has received an amazing level of worldwide attention, selling over 20 million copies. In it he wrote:

> . . . change your mental habits to belief instead of disbelief. Learn to expect, not to doubt. In so doing you bring everything into the realm of possibility . . . (including) that which has seemingly been impossible. . . . When you expect the best, you release a magnetic force in your mind, which by a law of attraction tends to bring the best to you. . . . It is amazing how a sustained expectation of the best sets in motion forces which cause the best to materialize.[47]

I suspect it is fair to say that Peale's popular book has been received by the public with a widely varying response. Some have considered the book to be a life-changing and revolutionary philosophy to live by. Others, with a more intellectual, scientific, and skeptical bent, have perhaps viewed Peale's positive thinking philosophy as being largely unrealistic and unsupported rhetoric.

However, over the years many of the elements of Peale's claims have gradually received support from experts and researchers. Recently a whole new research movement has emerged under the umbrella label "Positive Psychology" that shifts from the traditional focus on psychological dysfunction to positive considerations such as optimism, positive emotion, self-regulation, and well-being: that is, to what is right with people.[48] And this new movement has begun to have an impact in the work literature as well, involving researchers at prominent universities such as the University of Michigan and the University of Nebraska.[49]

The research and writings of prominent psychologist Martin Seligman on helplessness, pessimism, optimism, and now positive psychology, are probably the most visible body of work related to this recent emphasis. The jacket cover of his book *Learned Optimism* proclaims: "There is scientific evidence that optimism is vitally important in overcoming defeat, promoting achievement, and maintaining or improving health." Inside the book Seligman writes, "Optimism . . .can protect you against depression; it can raise your level of achievement; it can enhance your physical well-being; it is a far more pleasant mental state to be in."[50]

Peale himself viewed his work as scientifically sound and tried to connect it with contemporary knowledge, at least as it was understood in the early 1950s. For example, he cited preeminent psychologist William James who said, "Our belief at the beginning of a doubtful undertaking is the one thing that ensures the successful outcome of your venture."[51]

One of the more interesting recent applications of a similar philosophy has been in the area of manifestation. Authors Fred Fengler and Todd Varnum have described many cases involving people who have reportedly created outcomes in the physical world by willing and believing that they will occur. The accounts in their book *Manifesting Your Heart's Desire* are primarily based on a 20-person manifestation group that voluntarily agreed to meet for one year while setting aside the belief that much of their life experience was outside their control. The surprising reported experiences of the group resulting from their experimentation revealed wide-ranging outcomes including manifesting parking spaces, lost articles, mechanical repairs, athletic success, timely arrivals when running late, and even money and success in business.[52]

The essence of the primary elements for effective manifestation that the group discovered include the following:

~ Clarify what you want to manifest (your goals)

~ Use visualization (actually picture receiving what you want) and/or use verbal affirmations of receiving your desired outcome

~ Let go and detach from the outcome. Don't dwell on what you want, but rather simply trust that you will receive what is best for you regarding your goal

~ Be open to different possible forms that your desired outcome might take.

Though skeptical at first, I found the idea of manifesting to be fascinating, and I performed some simple experiments in my own life in an attempt to replicate some of their findings. As strange as it may sound, when I personally visualized something happening, and simply let go and trusted that I would receive the positive results I desired, I experienced occurrences that I cannot explain. I realize some readers may be skeptical about the results of some of these simple experiments I performed to test some of the manifesting group's results, but all I can say is that they happened. For example, when applying the principles I consistently found parking spaces in crowded locations where they are almost impossible to find.

I have also arrived exactly when I needed to for meetings when I was running very late and there was seemingly no way I could be on time. I simply pictured a time I wanted to arrive, did not check my watch but rather believed and pictured that I would be on time, and traveled at a safe comfortable speed. And almost magically, when I checked my watch just as I arrived where I needed to be, I was on time to the minute. And I repeated this experiment several times with a nearly perfect success rate when I was able to really believe it would happen and let go of the outcome.

If all this seems a little too mysterious and "new age-y," there are many ways that the manifesting power of positive thinking can be applied in very practical and more "left brain" logical ways. For example, the popular concept "Psycho-cybernetics," which centers on vividly imagining outcomes that you desire, has been widely used by athletes, entrepreneurs, managers, students, and many others to reach life goals. The original book titled *Psycho-Cybernetics* written by Maxwell Maltz has now sold over 30 million copies, and a new version was released in 2002 co-authored with Dan Kennedy.[53]

Maltz, who was a plastic surgeon, discovered in his practice that when he removed disfiguring scars from some of his patients, they still felt the inadequacy and flaws that had resulted from their past "ugly" physical appearance. Maltz concluded that the real scars were psychological

ones that affected the personality and that what really
needed to be changed was the self-image.

Psycho-cybernetics challenges us to stop the habit of
replaying past failures and instead purposefully replay our
successes in our mind, which over time will enhance our
self-image. Further, it calls for imagining in detail perfect
completion of activities, whether a golf swing, a speech, or
becoming a happy person. The approach suggests that
through repeated vivid positive imagination (taking time
out every day for this practice), our lives, our selves, and
our world are positively transformed. Psycho-cybernetics
is a practical approach that involves a choice to think more
positively (especially through mental images of our past
and our immediate performance) that millions of people
have used to manifest a better future.

Another more concrete example of the manifesting
power of positive thinking applies to the areas of feeling
lonely and in improving human relationships. Psychiatrist
and author Howard Cutler once asked the Dalai Lama, "Do
you ever get lonely?" The response was clear and simple,
"No." "No?" Cutler asked incredulously. "No," repeated
the Dalai Lama.[54]

The Dalai Lama then went on to explain that he looks
for the positive aspects of people, which helps him to connect with others. He also added that he has little fear that
his actions will cause people to view him with negative
judgment and that creates a kind of openness between him
and others. In particular, he advocated the value of compassion, which he says automatically changes your attitude
toward people. Relating to others with a spirit of compas-

sion will reduce fear, help establish a cordial atmosphere, and increase the chances of receiving an affectionate response.

I have also tried the same basic approach with many people over the years and have found the results to be very powerful. When I have purposely looked for the best in people and treated them with openness, respect, and a sense of compassion, I have been very pleased with the positive effects. I have often been surprised at the warm response I have received, even years later, when I had but a brief positive encounter with people so long before that I had completely forgotten about it.

The Dalai Lama has offered practical advice indeed. By approaching others in a positive and compassionate way we can actually create a more positive world for ourselves. In doing so we can establish the basis for rich and fulfilling relationships and largely eliminate loneliness in our lives all because of the manifesting power we release through our positive thinking based actions. This is perhaps one of the most potent secrets of emotional discipline. That is, when we choose to view the world through an optimistic and positive lens, we can actually unleash a force that helps to manifest the very world we choose to see.

Other Mind-Centered Emotional Discipline Choices

Use the following ideas to help create additional potential strategies that fit your particular needs.

~Use the *FROM* ➜ *TO mind technique* by drawing a line down the middle of a blank page and labeling the left column "FROM" and the right "TO." When you encounter upsetting situations in which you feel you are reacting poorly, record your current upsetting thoughts or beliefs about the situation in the left column and then replace them with more constructive thoughts/beliefs in the right column (e.g., FROM "this situation is hopeless" ➜ TO "this is a difficult challenge but I can handle it, I always do").[55]

~ Write *positive affirmations* on note cards that can help you cope with recurring upsetting situations. Read the cards when you encounter these situations and over time commit them to memory (e.g., "I am capable of responding to this situation in a calm and effective way").

~Use *visualization techniques* to rehearse constructive responses to recurring upsetting situations in your life

to help you prepare for when they occur (e.g., picture
yourself staying calm and responding effectively).

~Write down new *mental scripts* that you can "act out"
in your mind when you encounter difficult situations.
For example, prepare a short script for a cool and col-
lected theatrical character who stays calm and effective in emotionally charged situations, and "go into
character" with this script when you face challenging
situations.

~When you find yourself getting upset, *slowly count to
10 furry animals* (puppies, kittens, bunnies . . .), picturing the addition of one more of the playful little animals with each count.

~Practice *letting go of all judgment.* For example,
choose to just observe and appreciate everything that
you encounter without any evaluation or judgment.
Initially try this for a few minutes, then an hour at a
time, and eventually for an entire day or more.

~Try *living as though it is the last day of your life.* I know
we've all heard this idea before, but really try it, one
day at a time.

~How might you adapt the above ideas to create emotional discipline strategies that you can apply in your
life and work? What additional mind-centered
Emotional Discipline Choice ideas can you think of?

Our body is both a dwelling and a vehicle for life. When we treat it well, it will treat us well. When we treat it poorly, it will return the favor. We have great power to influence how we feel physically and thus the quality of our life experience. This power is founded on the amount and kind of care we choose to give our physical bodies each day.

Part Three

Body

~ ~ ~ ~ ~

He who has health has hope, and he who has hope has everything.

—Arabian proverb[56]

Physical fitness is an essential part of the best companies—and that includes CEOs. . . . Keeping fit has economic as well as spiritual and psychological benefits.

—T. Boone Pickens

Choice 14

Breathe with Healthful Discipline

~~~~~

. . .the breath is always here, right under our noses. You would think just by chance we might have come across its usefulness at one point or another.[57]

—Jon Kabat-Zinn

*L*et's start with a question: "What is the most powerful choice you can make to exercise emotional discipline through your body?" The surprising answer is *"Breathe!"* Of course you probably have already encountered the breathing challenge before in something you read, stress management training, health lectures, or wellness programs. It goes something like this.

> Yes, we all breathe, but we don't do it in the natural healthy way we were born to breathe. As babies we do it instinctively but somewhere in the course of growing up we learn to breathe in a restricted unhealthy way that is detrimental to our relaxation and health. The bottom line is that we need to relearn how to breathe in a healthy way and even more importantly do it on a regular basis in our daily lives.

It is fascinating that something so basic and seemingly automatic is such an important part of life and a key choice for exercising emotional discipline. The Time-Life home health book *The Medical Advisor,* for example, prescribes breathing exercises and techniques as health remedies or treatments for a wide range of physical problems including stress, anxiety, panic attack, emphysema, insomnia, and Parkinson's disease.[58]

So what are the secrets to this most basic of human functions? A source that I have found to be especially good for outlining alternative breathing techniques is the best-selling book by well-known natural and preventive health expert Andrew Weil, *Spontaneous Healing.*[59] Weil claims that the way we choose to breathe can enable us to regulate some of the most fundamental functions of our bodies such as digestion, heart rate, circulation, and blood pressure and consequently enhance our healing system. At the beginning of Chapter 9 on meditation I described one of the most basic and effective forms of breathing, abdominal breathing. Here I will provide examples for two additional practical and effective techniques, but I encourage you to explore other sources such as *Spontaneous Healing* for more advice on healthful breathing.

∼∼∼∼∼

It was the end of a long hectic day. Before he left for his home, Gerard lay quietly on a couch in his office. He knew that he could practice his breathing lying, sitting, or even standing, but since everyone else had already left the office and he was alone he decided to lie down. He began by touching his tongue to the upper roof of his mouth just above and behind his two front teeth, as he had learned in a yoga class. Then Gerard breathed in slowly and quietly through his nose to the count of four. He held his breath to the count of seven before exhaling slowly and audibly through his pursed lips to the count of eight.

He repeated this process eight complete cycles while his tongue continued to touch the point just behind and above his two front teeth. He knew that four cycles was usually enough to become much more relaxed, but today he felt he needed eight. After he completed this exercise Gerard returned to normal breathing and slowly sat up and prepared to leave for home, feeling much more relaxed and refreshed.

∼∼∼∼∼

Andrew Weil has prescribed this kind of breathing technique to many of his patients and describes it as a tonic for the nervous system. His patients report that it has cured a wide range of physical ailments from anxiety and stress to high blood pressure and cardiac arrhythmia. The following example describes yet another, less structured, type of breathing.

~ ~ ~ ~ ~

Marta sat quietly in her hotel room and practiced her breathing to prepare herself for the meeting she was about to attend. She wanted to center herself and calm her nerves before her important presentation. She began by concentrating on her exhalation, experiencing it as the beginning rather than the end of the breath cycle. She had learned from previous training that the musculature is stronger for controlling the out breath than for the inhalation. By concentrating on moving more air out of her lungs she automatically took in more air without even trying. This gently deepened her respiration, which increased her intake of oxygen and calmed her. She concentrated on pushing the air out of her lungs and letting her inhalation naturally follow for a few minutes until she felt relaxed, refreshed, and more focused.

~ ~ ~ ~ ~

These breathing techniques are just a couple of the many effective strategies that are available. By learning and practicing on a regular basis (preferably daily) healthy breathing methods that you find very beneficial, you can significantly *gain the power to choose how you feel*. So the next time you are struggling with a difficult situation that is bringing up challenging emotions, I encourage you to make the choice to *breathe with healthful discipline*.

Choice 15

Enhance Your Emotional Fitness Through Physical Fitness

~~~~~

Physical fitness is the basis for all other forms of excellence.

—John F. Kennedy

One fundamental way to improve the way we feel, and to increase our capacity to withstand emotional challenges, is to build and maintain our physical health. In my university classes I assign a term project to my students asking them to apply self-leadership strategies to work toward a personal improvement in some aspect of their life. A primary criterion for selecting their personal challenge topic is that it should be something that they view as significantly important to them. One of the most common areas students select to work on is their health, especially through nutrition and exercise. And by the end of the semester many of them report impressive results including lower stress, improved stamina, increased confidence, and in general feeling better about their lives.

As part of a new push to encourage fitness in the United States, a three-mile race was recently organized for 400 White House workers. President George W. Bush (55 years old) came in 26th place with the surprisingly brisk time for his age of 20 minutes 27 seconds. After the race he commented, "It's important for those of us in the White House to live how we talk. . . . If we're going to say we're going to live a healthy life, let's do it." And he went on to say to Americans in general, "I know you're a better worker if you exercise on a daily basis . . . you'll help keep the health care costs down . . . your life will be more complete."[60]

Indeed, health and fitness are now widely viewed as primary ingredients for a high-quality life, including, and perhaps especially, our work life. *The Wall Street Journal* recently published an entire section on health and fitness that proclaimed in large letters on the cover page: "Fitness isn't an option in today's sedentary lifestyle. For the first time in history, it's a must."[61] The list of executives who make fitness a key priority reads like a *Who's Who,* including Tom Monagham (founder of Domino's Pizza), Charles O. Rossotti (Commissioner of the IRS), Julian C. Day (CFO of Sears), Michael Magnum (President of the Magnum Group), and President George W. Bush.[62]

Most of us recognize that over time exercise can strengthen our bodies and help us to feel better. In fact, the documented benefits of exercise include improved circulation, more efficient functioning of the heart, strengthening of the respiratory system, enhancement of immune function, improvements in digestion, and facilitation of the body's elimination of metabolic wastes. It also stimulates the release of endorphins that fight depression and improve mood, neutralize stress, and promote relaxation and sounder sleep.[63]

Beyond exercise, we are also aware that our eating habits can have profound impacts on our quality of life. The common saying "you are what you eat" really drives this point home. What we eat can affect not only important physical factors such as our weight, heart health, blood pressure, digestion, susceptibility to allergies, and immune function, but also our mood. In her book *Food & Mood,* nutrition expert Elizabeth Somer describes in detail how food can have far-reaching impacts on the way we feel and, like a drug, can even act as a form of self-medication.[64]

So what are the basics of a good personal health plan? Dr. Tedd Mitchell, health columnist for *USA Today*

Weekend Magazine, prescribes straightforward ways for building better nutrition and exercise into our daily lives. The specific advice he offers may sound familiar, but it provides good practical guidance on yet another powerful choice for increasing the power to choose how you feel.[65]

To make *nutritional improvements,* create your own eating program with input from a spouse or friends who know you and can help you make sure your plan is realistic. Whenever possible, seek the advice of a registered dietitian. Include lots of vegetables and fruits, and emphasize low-fat high-fiber foods. Dr. Mitchell quotes a frequent statement of Dr. Kenneth Cooper, his colleague and founder of the prestigious Cooper Clinic, about the desirable number of daily servings of fruits and vegetables, "Five is fine but nine is divine." Mitchell also suggests keeping a daily log of your eating habits to track your progress (a favorite strategy of my students, by the way).

In terms of *exercise activity,* Dr. Mitchell prescribes a regime of moderate exercise for 30 minutes 5 days a week. The key is consistency. Exercise is something that should become a scheduled priority but kept realistic. Moderate exercise Monday through Friday is much more beneficial than overexerting a couple days a week with an intense workout. Again, Dr. Mitchell says keeping a log of your exercise activity is important so that you can track what you have, and have not, done on your exercise plan.

Probably one of the most helpful suggestions that Dr. Mitchell makes, because it frees us from trying to be a health perfectionist, is to follow what he calls "the 80/20 rule."[66] In its simplest form it suggests that we be "good" during the week but let our hair down on the weekend. He especially applies this rule to nutritional habits—eat well-balanced low-fat, high fruit and vegetable meals during the weekdays but starting Friday night, *enjoy!* He does suggest, even on the weekends, that we eat slowly with plenty of fluids but allow ourselves to (reasonably) indulge, even with an evening dessert and a glass of wine or mixed drink if we like. Then shift back to the healthy eating mode with the Sunday evening meal. And the same 80/20 rule could easily be applied to exercise as well—put in your daily 30 minutes of exercise during the week and then take the weekend off if you like.

Dr. Mitchell also prescribes good emotional health habits. Some of these include enjoying regular humor and laughter (more on this strategy in the next chapter), sharing your experiences with and helping others, being realistic about your goals at work, and finding a compelling purpose in your life that may have nothing to do with your job (art, travel, a hobby). However, those who have enjoyed the benefits that good healthy eating and exercise bring to their lives will confirm that these benefits in and of themselves go a long way toward building our emotional fitness. When we make the emotional discipline choice to eat well and exercise, we tend to feel good physically. And when we feel good physically, we tend to feel good about life in general.

Choice 16

Inner Jogging: Music and Laughter

~~~~~

Music hath charms to soothe the savage breast.

—William Congreve

Good humor makes all things tolerable.

—Henry Ward Beecher[67]

The previous chapter emphasized the importance of
choosing physical exercise as a means for enjoying a
fuller, healthier, and more emotionally rewarding life. For
many years the value of one specific form of cardiovascular
exercise—jogging—has been widely recognized. Unfortunately, the value of what I call "inner jogging" is not as
widely accepted. In particular, the powerful physical effects
of music and humor to positively condition and exercise
the body on the inside can be an important part of gaining
the ability to choose how you feel.

~ ~ ~ ~ ~

*As Andrew sat at his desk he noted that he was feeling
rather lethargic and in a blue mood. This concerned him because in 45 minutes he was scheduled to have an important
meeting with a very important client. Instinctively he reached
for his prerecorded tape of uplifting music. It contained inspiring theme songs from several of his favorite movies. Soon he
found his spirits lifted by the motivating music coming
through his headphones, and he felt enthused about the
prospects for his meeting.*

~ ~ ~ ~ ~

Music is one of the most helpful tools available for affecting the way we feel. It can calm us, lift our spirits, make
us feel sad, or pump us up for life's battles. By studying different types of music and the effects they have on our bodies we can effectively draw upon music as we need it.

Movie themes, for example, are often designed for the emotional uplifting impact that they have on audiences. By purchasing favorite sound tracks, or even better, recording our favorite songs from different movie sound tracks, we can always have available to us a healthy uplifting choice to influence the way we feel without having to resort to caffeine or other drugs.

Other types of music can have calming effects. Classical baroque music performed in a slow steady beat can help us to become calmer and more open to learning new information. And if you want to experience overall positive physical effects that seem to tune the body and mind and create an overall greater sense of well-being, it appears that Mozart should be a key composer of choice. The subtitle of the popular book *The Mozart Effect* by author Don Campbell summarizes the vast potential of the power of music, and especially music written by Mozart, for affecting our physical experience—*Tapping the Power of Music to Heal the Body, Strengthen the Mind, and Unlock the Creative Spirit.*[68]

To effectively tap the potential of music to enrich the way we feel, the developers of the audiotape program *Optimal Health,* Jim Loehr, Nick Hall, and Jack Groppel, suggest that we prepare at least two customized audiotapes (each about 12 to 15 minutes long), one with uplifting inspiring music and the other with calming recovery music.[69] And I suggest adding a third tape consisting of some favorite Mozart music excerpts (or selections of other classical composers of his time period if you don't care for Mozart). Then simply select the music you need based on the way you're feeling. To keep your tapes effective, it is wise to update them every few weeks so that they provide new fresh stimulation.

Equally important is the choice to include humor in your life. One of the most noteworthy accounts of the power of humor is told in the book *Head First* by Norman Cousins.[70] Rather than choosing despair and hopelessness in the face of cancer, Cousins called on the power of humor to help him overcome the obstacles he faced. His book describes how humor affected his body in profound healing ways.

Laughter has been found to work many muscles and provide healthful exercise in some ways similar to physical exercise at a gym. Writer and trainer C. W. Metcalf, who specializes in promoting the many benefits of humor for our work and lives, emphasizes to his clients the important scientific medical findings of psychoneuroimmunology (PNI).[71] PNI examines the interaction between the mind and body, drawing from the fields of psychology, neurology, and immunology. Our perceptions of what is happening to us in life affect important physiological processes in the body that can dramatically affect our health.

For example, Metcalf points out that it can be difficult for our physiology to distinguish between a threat to our ego (for instance, when we are embarrassed or criticized) and an actual threat to our life. And perceived threats trigger the well-known "fight or flight stress response," which over time can produce very unhealthy consequences. On the other hand, if we learn to lighten up, keep a sense of humor, and experience laughter regularly, and the positive thoughts and emotions associated with them, these choices can actually impact our brain chemistry and our immune system in very positive ways.

Laughter is good for us. By intentionally choosing to surround ourselves with humorous books, tapes, and DVDs, we can provide ourselves with the healthful injection that we need to get through the difficult times and make the goods times seem even better.

Searching for the humor in even the most difficult of circumstances at work or in our personal lives can also help us to be more balanced and better able to cope. And this can contribute to our personal effectiveness. Sam Walton, founder of the phenomenally successful Wal-Mart stores, included humor and fun as a primary ingredient in his business success philosophy:

> Find some humor in your failures. Don't take yourself so seriously. Loosen up, and everybody around you will loosen up. Have fun. Show enthusiasm—always. When all else fails, put on a silly costume and sing a silly song. Then make everybody else sing with you. . . . All this is more important, and more fun, than you think, and it really fools the competition. "Why should we take those cornballs at Wal-Mart seriously?"[72]

The idea is not to shirk your responsibilities and to avoid facing difficult problems but rather to choose humor as an important strategy for emotional discipline. Together, music and humor can provide you with an effective inner jogging regime that can help you maintain the health of your body. The conscious choice to listen to uplifting and calming music as needed and to enjoy the humor of life with a good dose of laughter can provide a potent combination for gaining the power to choose how you feel.

Choice 17

Body Work 101:
Massage and Beyond

~~~~~

Body work is an umbrella term for the many techniques,
both ancient and modern, that promote relaxation and
treat ailments through lessons in proper movement,
postural reeducation, exercise, massage, and various
forms of bodily manipulation.

—The Medical Advisor, Time-Life Books[73]

There are many healthy and enjoyable body-centered choices that you can make every day to practice emotional discipline. In this chapter I will share some body work possibilities that involve receiving therapeutic "manipulative" treatments, such as massage, from trained professionals. In the next chapter I will address body work via healthful forms of physical movement such as Tai Chi.

~ ~ ~ ~ ~

It had been a long day and Alicia felt tight and tense as she drove out of the parking lot. She was not going directly home today; instead she had scheduled one of her favorite self-renewing activities. Soon she found herself relaxing face down on a padded table as her masseuse began to work on her neck and shoulders with a firm kneading technique. This was Alicia's favorite part. She focused on every relaxing and pleasurable sensation, vividly logging the experience into her memory for future use when stress would strike again. And as she drifted into deeper and deeper levels of relaxation, she could feel her muscles completely let go as the stress seemed to drain out of her entire body.

A few months earlier, when Alicia had her first session, she had been a little uncomfortable about the idea of having a massage, but now she made it a point to schedule one twice a month. In fact, massage had become an important priority to her no matter how busy her schedule seemed to be.

She found massage to be like a reset button for her that helped her to be more relaxed, renewed, reinvigorated, better balanced, and more effective in her work and life. When she felt especially stressed, whether during a tense meeting or while flying through a turbulent thunderstorm on a plane, she found that she could calm herself by reconnecting, through her imagination, with the relaxed feeling she experienced during a massage.

~ ~ ~ ~ ~

Massage is one of the most basic and effective forms of body work. It can be an important choice for applying emotional discipline in a practical way. The key, as with the other emotional discipline strategies in this book, is to make the choice and act on it. Ask colleagues and friends for recommendations of a competent masseuse, and then pick up the phone and schedule an appointment. After you give massage a fair try (perhaps two or three appointments), if you verify that it does bring significant benefits, you can choose to make it a priority in your life, build the cost into your budget, and schedule regular appointments.

My own experience with massage has been that it is very beneficial for reducing excess stress, muscle tension, and creating an overall sense of well-being. And it can be a catalyst for emotional release. Typically, I have received a combination of mild to moderate muscle massage combined with some acupressure. *Acupressure* is a technique (usually associated with Chinese medicine) that "involves pressing points on the body with fingers or hands to alter the internal flow of a supposed vital force or energy called *chi*, strengthening it, calming it, or removing a blockage of the flow."[74]

Stronger treatments related to massage therapy are available for those who are comfortable with more invasive body work. For example, *shiatsu*, a Japanese healing art that is similar in some ways to acupressure, involves firm finger pressure (that can seem uncomfortable at first) applied to points of the body to balance energy. It is intended to help eliminate pain and promote healing benefits. *Rolfing* is an invasive and more intense form of body work that focuses on the connective tissue that covers the muscles (fascia), with the intent of bringing the body back into correct alignment. While massage generally has the capacity to unleash some of the stored emotional tension held in our bodies, this is particularly true of rolfing. I personally went through a series of rolfing sessions and found the process to be uncomfortable some of the time during the treatment, but it seemed to produce more lasting feelings of healthy release than regular massage.

Within the variety of massage alternatives, many are considerably less expensive and less physically demanding, and can be self-applied. These include electronic massagers that can be easily researched on the Internet or even tried out in many of the stores that carry them. Some send rhythmic vibrations or provide therapeutic thumping sensations into your back and shoulders, and others have deep kneading nodules that provide a more intense massage on targeted muscle groups.

It is also fairly simple to learn and work with the various acupressure points on the body to address your symptoms directly.[75] For example, if you feel anxious, one point to work with is called Pericardium 6. You may experience relief by gently but firmly pressing your thumb in the center of your inner wrist two finger widths from the crease in your wrist and between your two forearm bones. Continue pressure for one minute, three to five times, and then repeat on the other wrist.[76]

An important part of emotional discipline involves discovering and choosing to apply treatments that promote positive health and feelings of well-being in your body. Through experimentation, your body will give you the feedback you need to help you decide what is right for you. Finding alternatives that provide the results you seek, whether they be relaxing or invigorating benefits, and then choosing them as an important part of your emotional discipline practices, is well worth the effort and search.

Choice 18

Body Work 102: Tai Chi Movement and More

~~~~~

I became very ill . . . because of years of hard work and vigorous schedules. My doctor told me that my condition was incurable using available medication. . . . At the same time, one of my friends . . . told me about Tai Chi . . . for three years, I practiced. . . . In only two weeks, my appetite improved and the frequency and severity of my stomach pain lessened . . . (eventually) my stomach was completely healed . . . my heart returned to normal, and I regained total good health without the use of drugs.

—Jou, Tsung-Hwa[77]

Most contemporary views on physical fitness prescribe a combination of aerobic exercise, strength
training, and stretching and flexibility. My own experience
with fitness, growing up in the United States, centered on
competitive sports. Through high school I actively partici-
pated in football, wrestling, and track each year. Much of
the focus was on developing endurance and strength
through a rather aggressive form of training. My memories
are filled with screaming coaches, exhausting drills, rivers
of sweat, and many bruises and muscle strains.

I am grateful for much of what I learned about discipline and competition through sports. At the same time I
often marvel at how my personal needs for maintaining
good health and well-being as an adult are so different
from what I was taught as a youth. I regret that I did not receive training on how to relax, gently exercise, and care for
my body in a more centered and balanced way. It was years
later before I discovered the value and benefits of meditation and fitness activities as practiced in China and other
countries in the East, which combine healthy breathing
with fluid and relaxed body movements. I enjoyed vast
benefits when I finally discovered and added some *Eastern
moves* to my Western fitness activities.

I have subsequently received training in a variety of
activities originating from the far East including yoga,
Qigong (pronounced *chee kung*), and Tai Chi. I highly recommend that anyone sincerely interested in a lifetime of
health benefits explore these alternative physical well-
being practices. Such alternative forms of exercise devote a
great deal of attention to creating a balanced approach to

physical health, combining relaxation, meditation, and healthy breathing. By mentally focusing attention on different parts of the body that are being slowly moved and stretched, combined with relaxation and deep slow abdominal breathing, our natural physical healing processes are released. Stress seems to melt away while the body is slowly strengthened and made more flexible.

I especially recommend regular practice of a basic set of Qigong exercises and/or Tai Chi (which is actually a special standing and moving form of Qigong), but I know many people who have benefited a great deal from practicing yoga or other similar forms of exercise on a regular basis as well. Most people have some awareness of yoga, which involves a variety of independent slow movements and relatively static poses that stretch, bend, and twist the body, combined with deep breathing. Lesser known is the practice of Qigong, an ancient Chinese system of exercise similar to yoga, that helps reduce stress and promote health and fitness.[78] Qi means life energy and Qigong can be defined as "energy exercise" or "breath work."[79]

I have taken classes in Qigong and Tai Chi, a 2,000-year-old Chinese martial art that is steadily increasing in popularity in the United States as well as many other parts of the world.[80] Unlike popular images of high-action self-defense oriented martial arts, Tai Chi involves a peaceful, relaxing, yet strengthening set of movements that are performed in a continuous fluid sequence. Its benefits include promoting health, reducing stress, creating harmony of mind, improving balance and coordination, increasing strength, and rejuvenation and longevity. The only rub is that Tai Chi can be challenging to master, requiring several months to years to learn all the correct postures and techniques of one complete form. However, significant benefits are gained throughout the learning process, which itself can be very enjoyable and rewarding.

Of course many variations on these practices are available, and many books, audio and videotapes, and DVDs can help guide your progress. For example, I have found one book to be especially effective for introducing the basics of Qigong in a way that is easy to learn and build into daily living (requiring as little as six minutes a day for a complete rejuvenating feel-good light workout): *QiGong for Beginners* by Stanley Wilson.[81] Even better, most communities offer adult or continuing education courses that can teach you the basics.

My most recent training resulted when I joined a local Tai Chi center and took classes about once a week for several months to refine and improve my practice. I often practice the basic Tai Chi form that I have learned (a variation of the yang short form) in the early morning when I first get up and/or in the evening when I am winding down from the day. I sometimes do a short warm-up with some simple Qigong exercises (along the lines of those explored in the book *QiGong for Beginners* mentioned above) followed by Tai Chi. Together these exercises take about 15 minutes.

I especially enjoy practicing the form in a natural setting (such as by a lake, forest, or the ocean) in the early morning when the sun is rising. But I find a Tai Chi break to be refreshing and rejuvenating any time of day and in most any location that provides a modest amount of private space (even an area as small as 6 by 10 feet), especially when I feel stressed, anxious, or sluggish.

If you are searching for a relaxing way to strengthen your body and improve your overall health throughout your adult years, I highly recommend that you look beyond Western forms of exercise. I still enjoy more traditional Western activities such as hiking, jogging, biking, swimming, and moderate weight training. Nevertheless, the benefits that I have gained from yoga, and especially Qigong and Tai Chi, have greatly enriched and balanced my fitness activities. They provide a great way to choose to feel good and can provide benefits not only for the body, but also for the mind, emotions, and spirit. They simultaneously contribute to physical strength while removing stress and creating a calm healthy center for interacting with the world, which can be very beneficial when facing emotionally challenging situations. I hope you too will incorporate some "Eastern Moves" into your life.

Choice 19

Flow with Balance

~~~~~

*The three men were called crafters and worked side
by side. The first man thought the sun was too hot,
his tools were too old, and that his arms got too tired.
He frowned and grumbled as he worked.
The second thought of the money and praise he would
receive for his work, and of being promoted to chief
crafter one day. He did not think about his work
much at all—only of his better future ahead.
The third man focused on the creativity of his design,
the feeling of power and strength he enjoyed as he
worked his tools, and of the admiration he felt for the
finely shaped item he was creating with his own hands.
He smiled, for he was not working at all.*[82]

*B*alance and moderation are often offered as the keys to a long, healthy, and rewarding life. Certainly excess in food, drink, and other indulgences can lead us to self-defeating ends. And the idea that workaholism and other compulsions and obsessions can be destructive forces in our lives is widely recognized. But finding true healthy balance probably has less to do with simply abstaining from excess and more to do with finding meaningful work and activities that help us to experience the authentic life we feel most meant to live. So how can we avoid the tendency toward imbalance and instead choose to live and work in ways that are more healthy, constructive, motivating, fulfilling, and yes, balanced?

One potent answer to this question is contained in the concept of *flow* developed by Mihaly Csikszentmihalyi. While largely centered on our state of consciousness, flow has significant implications for our physical experience as well. For example, people generally experience less pain (or no pain at all), despite having physical injuries or other painful conditions, when they are deeply involved with an activity and in a state of flow.[83] The essence of the flow experience is captured in Mihaly Csikszentmihalyi's words:

> "Flow" is the way people describe their state of mind when consciousness is harmoniously ordered, and they want to pursue whatever they are doing for its own sake.
>
> The optimal state of inner experience is one in which there is order in consciousness. This happens when psychic energy—or attention—is invested in realistic

goals, and when skills match the opportunities for action. The pursuit of goals brings order in awareness because a person must concentrate attention on the task at hand and momentarily forget everything else. These periods of struggling to overcome challenges are what people find to be the most enjoyable times of their lives. A person who has achieved control over psychic energy and has invested it in consciously chosen goals cannot help but grow into a more complex being. By stretching skills, by reaching toward higher challenges, such a person becomes an increasingly extraordinary individual.[84]

Csikszentmihalyi has compared many aspects of flow to the practice of hatha yoga, which helps practitioners achieve "a joyous self-forgetful involvement through concentration which . . . is made possible through discipline of the body."[85]

The key to incorporating flow into our life experiences is centered on the idea of nurturing the "autotelic" aspect of our personality and engaging in "autotelic" activities. Csikszentmihalyi has explained that the word *autotelic* combines "two Greek roots: 'auto' (self) and 'telos' (goal)."[86] We can experience more flow by increasing our capacity to perform activities for their own value rather than in pursuit of a separate external reward or outcome. In this process we can obtain the related experience of timelessness.[87] We transcend our sense of time and self and become fully immersed in our present-moment activity. This transcendence can release not only a sense of joy but our deeper creativity. By seeking out those activities that we can value experiencing for their own sake, where our main goal is engaging in the activity, we can increase the level of flow in our lives.

On a bit larger scale, all this points to the importance of finding work that we can truly believe in, that is of significant value in its own right, that is worthy of being our life work. A senior vice president in a large utility discussed what he sees as the important future role of companies—to help employees discover the work that is most meaningful to them. He explained, ". . . if you had a company in which all the people were doing their life's work, you would have more loyalty, more resilience, more creativity, more innovation and a deeper sense of self-reliance, self-renewal, and self-generation."[88]

Richard Brodie has described his own career experience in a way that brings to light how empty work and life can be in the absence of any meaningful sense of flow. He put it this way, "I was Microsoft's most golden of Golden Boys! At the age of 26 I had written one of the world's best-selling pieces of software, worked personally with one of the smartest and most famous people on the planet (Bill Gates), and had enough stock options to make me a millionaire . . . (but) I was unhappier and under more stress than I had ever been in my life."[89]

He recounted how his high performance in taking the lead on the initial version of Microsoft Word landed him a promotion from Bill Gates, including management of a brand new department. He explained that he had gone from a job in which he was world-class to one in which he was unqualified and felt incompetent. No longer was his focus on the pure performance of his job but instead on fear of being found out as incapable of performing his new responsibilities. In essence he had lost all sense of flow in his work, and his career and life had swung widely out of balance. His self-esteem plummeted and he quit his job.

After a three-year search to find himself, he discovered "The key to self-esteem: to spend every moment of life pursuing what's most important to you." Eventually he did go back to Microsoft and created his own position—a kind of special agent who came in and helped save the day when projects were faltering and looked nearly hopeless. Obviously he had created a job that was very challenging, but it was one he was able to throw himself into with a sense of competence and passion for the work itself. In doing so he rediscovered his personal effectiveness, contributing to the huge success of Windows and the database program Access, among other projects. Although he worked longer hours than he ever had, he worked with far greater effectiveness and satisfaction. He explained that he was now able to face every day knowing that he was working on what was most important to him with a sense of authenticity in his work.

Flow can be a powerful part of an emotionally disciplined life. When we are in a state of flow, our emotional difficulties seem to simply vanish. We are so fully engaged in our immediate activity that worries and concerns fade out of our consciousness.

Here are three specific suggestions to help you choose flow for your life:

~Set challenging but achievable worthwhile goals and work toward them.

~Seek out challenging activities that you believe in, that interest you, and that will stretch your perform-ance abilities and help you learn and grow.

~Try to strike a middle ground between difficulty and easiness, arousal and boredom, and anxiety and relax-ation.

In the end, one of the wisest choices you can make is to seek balance in the various aspects of your life. This even suggests the need to *discipline your discipline*. Emotional discipline offers a life-changing doorway to a more fulfilling and meaningful life, but working too hard at it can be as dysfunctional as ignoring it all together. As you continue to make healthy choices that can help you gain in power to choose how you feel, be both firm and gentle with yourself. Seek reasonable levels of practice and don't get hung up on perfection. Challenge yourself, make an honest effort to select healthy choices, and then let go and flow to wherever it leads you.

Other Body-Centered Emotional Discipline Choices

~ *Travel to places that encourage plenty of walking and hiking.* Many places in the world automatically tend to trigger more walking (e.g., in many towns in Europe walking is a primary way to get around) or have very beautiful inviting places to hike (e.g., U.S. National Parks).

~ *Try the all-around physical conditioning program referred to as **Pilates*** (named after its creator, Joseph H. Pilates), which focuses on the "core" muscles of the abdomen but is designed to strengthen, lengthen, tone, and increase flexibility in your entire body. Many books, tapes, and fitness centers are available that can help you get started.

~ *Take a class or read a book on healthy cooking.* Then try preparing at least one very healthy but very tasty meal per week and increase the frequency over time. Develop a hobby of healthy food preparation and eating.

~ *Take up a new outdoor (or at least active) hobby.* This could be birdwatching, backpacking, camping, spelunking, rock climbing, or any other new undertaking that encourages healthy exercise.

~*Participate regularly in a new sport,* or one you have discontinued (if it includes significant increased levels of exertion for you, it would be wise to have a health checkup with your doctor first). Some good choices include playing basketball, joining a softball team, jogging, biking, cross-country skiing, golf, tennis, swimming, and ice skating.

~*Ask around and locate health food restaurants in your area noted for preparing delicious meals* and then try them out. Get in the habit of seeking special enjoyable dining out experiences that are good for you.

~*Run errands on foot or via a bike* if possible. If this is not practical for you, then try parking in the more re-mote spaces of parking lots to increase your walking. Don't fight for the "good spaces" close to the stores, go for the less popular ones farther out.

~*Get in the habit of taking the stairs* instead of the elevator.

~If you have the flexibility in your workplace, *take a walk when you need to think over projects and challenges* that need your creative and problem-solving ca-pability. Bring a pen and paper so that you can capture new ideas that occur to you as you walk.

~How can you adapt the above ideas to create emo-tional discipline strategies that you can apply in your life and work? What additional body-centered Emotional Discipline Choice ideas can you think of?

The ultimate life choices are rooted in the spirit. Our best selves are often hidden by our daily habits and activities. When we take the time to stop, relax, and listen deep within, our whole world takes on a new more satisfying dimension. A choice to awaken and nurture the spirit is a choice to feel and be better throughout our lives.

~~~~~~~~~~~~

Part Four

Spirit

~ ~ ~ ~ ~

There are only two forces in the world,
the sword and the spirit. In the long run the sword
will always be conquered by the spirit.

—Napoleon Bonaparte[90]

Choice 20

The Power of Silence

~~~~~

Speech is silver, silence is golden.

—French Proverb[91]

One of life's interesting ironies is that silence, often associated with passivity, is such a potent force. Silence can help us become centered, calm, introspective, and perhaps even wise. And silence can often get our point across much more effectively than the most persuasive argument.

First, consider how important silence is for learning. When we speak, it is difficult to learn more than what we already know. But when we silently listen to what others have to say, whole new worlds are available to us. We can begin to understand things from the perspectives of others, and we can have access to what they know that we don't. As we listen to the concerns and opinions of others, we are freed, for a time, from worrying about our own self-focused problems and we can learn a bit about what it would be like to be in someone else's circumstances. Silently listening holds the key to a fuller, more informed, and empathetic experience of life.

Although silence may seem uncomfortable at first for those who are used to constant noise, and perhaps especially for significant extroverts, it offers valuable gifts for those who learn how to use it well. Even when we encounter conflicts in which we decide we must take a stand, silence can be a powerful ally to help us achieve our ends. In Chapter 6 on emotional kung fu, some of the advice offered in the book *Getting to Yes* was shared concerning negotiations. The authors Fisher and Ury also persuasively argue for the use of silence:

> Silence is one of your best weapons. . . if they made an
> unreasonable proposal or an attack you regard as un-

justified, the best thing to do may be to sit there and not say a word. . . . If you have asked an honest question to which they have provided an insufficient answer, just wait. People tend to feel uncomfortable with silence, particularly if they have doubts about the merits of something they have said.

Obviously Fisher and Ury see silence as a powerful negotiating tool that often is much more effective than actively trying to explain or argue for your position. They continue,

> Silence often creates the impression of a stalemate which the other side will feel impelled to break by answering your question or coming up with a new suggestion. When you ask questions, pause. Don't take them off the hook . . . Some of the most effective negotiating you will ever do is when you are not talking."[92]

Silence offers yet another valuable treasure—it provides the opportunity for us to listen to ourselves. At the outset of this chapter I pointed out that when we talk we limit our opportunity to learn from others. Nevertheless, we can also learn to listen to ourselves in a new, more effective way, to hear what our inner voice has to teach us. Author Parker Palmer put it this way, "We listen for guidance everywhere except from within. . .(we believe) that simply because we have said something, we understand what it means. But often we do not . . . we need to listen to what our lives are saying and take notes on it, lest we forget our own truth. . . ."[93]

This idea suggests a different kind of silence. It might be an intentional silencing of our mind from its usual chatter while we are speaking and looking for the deeper lessons in what we are saying. Or it might be choosing periods of silent reflection to concentrate on what our mind has to say silently within.

To bring to life some of the primary themes of the power of silence, imagine the following exchange between Susan and her co-worker Tom, who normally treats her with ongoing hostility.

~ ~ ~ ~ ~

"You've done it again, Susan. Your planned agenda for our upcoming department meeting hardly even acknowledges the work I am doing on the new customer service program. I don't care if it is your turn to plan the agenda, you are obviously acting in a self-serving way and snubbing my hard work!"

Susan felt emotion welling up inside of her. Her immediate reaction was to view Tom's comments as an attack on her personally, simply because he didn't like her. But she resisted the temptation to attack him back, as she normally would have, out of anger. Instead she went silent and let her mind and emotions settle down while looking squarely at Tom with an expression that indicated she was giving him her full attention.

A few moments went by and Tom began to shift uncomfortably. Meanwhile, Susan thought about the agenda and how she had purposely scheduled Tom's review of his new program for last so that it could receive full attention once other more routine department details were out of the way. She did in fact feel that the program was important and had specifically scheduled it in a way she thought would best allow it undivided attention. "It must be that Tom is upset about being scheduled for last," she concluded silently in her mind, "but I need to verify this to be sure that I understand his concerns."

Finally, Tom spoke again, now sounding less sure than before. "Well, what bothers me is that you scheduled me as the very last item on the agenda. Don't you think my work is important enough to deserve more priority?" Tom finished, now sounding more hostile again.

Once again, Susan paused for a few moments as she allowed any defensiveness she felt to ease and reflected on what Tom had said. She calmly studied his growing uneasiness. Finally, she spoke, noticing a slight look of relief on Tom's face. "On the contrary, Tom, I think your work on the new program is very important. That is why I scheduled it as the main focus of the meeting after all the routine department details have been considered."

"Oh," Tom responded simply.

A few more moments passed and Tom continued, "I guess I might have jumped to conclusions."

Tom now stared at Susan, expecting some kind of acknowledgment to what he thought was an indirect apology on his part.

Susan remained silent but attentive.

"Sorry about that. Thanks for scheduling it so it won't get lost in the details," Tom heard himself saying even to his own surprise as he began to see the logic in what Susan had done and wished to end the tension he felt.

"That's OK, Tom. Glad to help," Susan responded and then returned to her attentive silence.

"OK, see you at the meeting," Tom said as his voice trailed off and he left Susan's office with a combined expression of relief and a little confusion.

~~~~~

Choosing silence can introduce a beneficial force in our lives. It can be a primary tool for enjoying more effective communication, enhanced learning, meaningful personal growth, peace, more effective relationships, and enriched feelings about our life and our work.

Choice 21

The Drama of Subtlety

~~~~~

We can do no great things—
only small things with great love.

—Mother Teresa[94]

We have a natural tendency to pay close attention and react to the large dramatic events in our lives. All too often these dramatic influences are quite negative. Career failures, relationship breakdowns, and major illnesses are obvious examples. And big problems at work, significant interpersonal conflicts, and difficult financial setbacks capture our attention and impact our feelings as well. Together these potentially demoralizing forces can drag our spirits downward.

Meanwhile, the more subtle, positive but less obvious, events in our lives often are not even noticed. Nevertheless, they too can play a dramatic role in how we experience life if we become attuned to them. The idea that the small things in life may hold great potency for bearing much good was elegantly brought to life in the New Testament.

> The kingdom of heaven is like a mustard seed that someone took and sowed in his field; it is the smallest of all the seeds, but when it has grown it is the greatest of shrubs and becomes a tree, so that the birds of the air come and make nests in its branches.—Matthew 13:31-32, New Revised Standard Version

It seems even heaven is based on the drama of subtlety.

These insights raise a tremendous opportunity for choosing how we feel. By making a choice to be proactively sensitive to all the magnificent subtlety in the world, we can place ourselves on a path that can uplift our whole experience of life. Albert Schweitzer said, "In everyone's life at some time our inner fire goes out. It is then burst into flame by an encounter with another human being. We should all be thankful for those people who rekindle the inner spirit." Of course, the challenge that could be thrown back in response to this encouraging proclamation is "what if the person who can rekindle my spirit never shows up?" The good news is that we can be that person for ourselves if we learn and choose to be open to the positive drama of subtlety.

William Blake wrote poignant words that illustrate these ideas well:

> To see a world in a grain of sand
> and a heaven in a wild flower,
> hold infinity in the palm of your hand
> and eternity in an hour.

—the drama of subtlety indeed.

It is unfortunate that sometimes our large expectations can get in the way of our ability to feel good about our lives. We may want a dramatic expression of love from a personal partner. We might expect a large pay raise or to be presented with significant public recognition and awards for our work. We may, perhaps without realizing it, be expecting others to be more concerned about our immediate needs than their own. And we may want and expect these large dramatic things, and want them now!

As a consequence we can miss the small but heartfelt gesture that a family member does specifically for our benefit. Or we might not notice the sincere but subtle compliment someone offers us at work. And we may miss the "olive branch" compromise that long-time opponents offer on a subject that here-to-now they have been unbudging on. And these examples don't even begin to address the vast miracles in the world that surround us every day, such as the beautiful blue sky on a sunny day or the gentle breeze that lightly strokes our hair. Or perhaps they take the form of the colorful bird that serenades us or the exotic butterfly that graciously points out the most beautiful flower by alighting on it.

Sometimes, when we are really caught up in what seem to be the bigger cares of life, the drama of subtlety may even seek us out and offer us the gift of freedom, if only for a moment, from our many self-imposed burdens. The story below describes one person's remarkable encounter with one of nature's tinier creatures.

Hummingbird Moments

Sometimes everything on the list doesn't get checked off. Sometimes things just don't get done.

It was late August. With Christmas-like excitement about seeing family and friends, we were almost frantically getting ready for a week in Idaho. Our flight was at 2:15. My husband was at work managing last minute leaving-details, and I had half a day to nurture all of our flora and fauna and pack the necessaries for travel to Idaho. I'd taken the dog for a romp in the woods, set the sprinklers with timers to keep the flowers joyful, tidied the house, mowed the grass, filled the

bird/squirrel feeders, loved on the cats, and showed
the neighbors how to keep everyone alive and happy.

Watering the garden on our deck, I mentally
checked my to-do list. Holding the hose on a hibiscus,
I froze as a tiny forest friend flew to the hummingbird
feeder and dipped and drank until satisfied. Just as
quickly as she came, she turned to go back to the tree-
tops and, with missile-speed, she flew directly into the
sun-sky-forest reflection on the glass door. She fell to
the deck like a pebble.

I tiptoed over to the tiny victim of civilization and
slowly knelt beside her. Moving one muscle fiber at a
time, I picked her up. There was not even a flicker as
she lay on her side, covering barely half of my palm.
Gently, ever, ever so gently, I began stroking her breast
with one finger. I was awed by the dazzling ruby
feather on her throat as I admired God's handiwork in
the jewel-like prismatic reflections of sunshine from
her tiny feathers.

Moments crawled. Edging over to sit on the bench
under the overhanging trees, I continued to stroke for,
oh . . . I don't know how long. By then, time didn't
matter.

Finally, there was a gentle flicker—a feather flutter
as she struggled to right herself. For a time she was
contented to rest in the nest of my hand. Her eyes
dragged open and we met. We held a whispered conversation. She found her feet and stood, stretched her
wings, and nestled down again. Time passed. She

stretched again . . . . tried flight . . . . staggered to my
forearm. Rest . . . . a scramble to my shoulder . . . .
rest . . . . a lunge to the deck railing . . . . rest . . . . and
then she rose, hovered, and darted into the canopy of
green.

It was then I who was motionless. I just sat, waiting . . . listening . . . watching . . . hoping . . . for just
one more touch. Tears began to flow. . . and then a
buzz crossed my ear. The tiny bird hovered, looking
me straight in the eyes. Gently, I moved my hand up-
ward, holding out one finger . . . She perched . . . . but
this time for just a hummingbird moment . . . . as if to
say "Thank you!" And then she was gone.

That afternoon as we, too, took flight, I reflected
on the morning's script . . . . a woman, a schedule, a
list , ... and a God who sent a hummingbird to remind me that, even in the busiest of times, I must take
time to stop . . . . to wait . . . . to listen . . . . to watch
. . . . to let nothing else matter . . . . and then to say
"Thank you!"

Sometimes everything on the list doesn't get
checked off. Sometimes things just don't get done.
Sometimes . . .

When we are sincerely committed to making a choice
to open ourselves to uplifted feelings, we will discover that
we are surrounded by countless potential collaborators,

both in the natural and human-created world. In this sense feeling good truly is a choice we make from moment to moment. While we may not be able to feel great every moment, we can choose to search for the subtle gifts in our lives that often represent and produce significant, even dramatic, good feelings. We can discover the vast array of kindness and miraculous forces in the world. Those who truly make the emotional discipline choice to commit to feeling good are called to search every day for all the dramatic subtlety that is capable of rekindling our inner spirit.

Choice 22

The Power of Purpose

~ ~ ~ ~ ~

Ever more people today have the means to live,
but no meaning to live for.

—Viktor Frankl[95]

Difficult challenges and difficult feelings are an inevitable part of life. Sometimes things can seem so dark and gloomy that it may be all we can do just to carry on with our work and lives. These times are especially challenging when our efforts lack a sense of purpose. Eventually we must all face the questions: "What has my life contributed of lasting value? What was it all about? Why was I here at all?" And when these times come, we will be greatly aided if we have exercised the emotional discipline to harness the *power of purpose*.

In his book *The Power of Purpose,* Richard Leider wrote:

> Purpose is that deepest dimension within us—our central core or essence—where we have a profound sense of who we are, where we came from, and where we're going. Purpose is the quality we choose to shape our lives around. Purpose is a source of energy and direction.[96]

Indeed, when life is its most challenging, we need a sense of meaning and purpose to provide us with the energy and direction that can help us sustain ourselves. But what can provide us with the sense of purpose we need? One primary source of purpose is service to others that is driven by an altruistic spirit. For those who might question the realism of prescribing altruistic service as a valuable source of finding meaningful purpose in our seemingly self-centered world, a creative perspective on the subject was proposed years ago.

The well-known author Hans Selye, in his classic writings on human stress, coined the term "altruistic egoism." Selye argued that by helping others (altrusim) and "earning their love" while at the same time recognizing our own needs and enhancing ourselves (egoism) we can enjoy a rewarding lifestyle, free of disabling stress. He explained that we possess a natural biological drive toward self-preservation. Consequently, according to Selye, it is only through marrying this "self-centered" nature with altruistic efforts to win the goodwill of others, that a happy meaningful life will result.[97]

One avenue for manifesting this kind of purpose in our lives is through our life work. The best-selling author and influential contemporary poet, David Whyte, who has consulted and made presentations for many Fortune 500 corporations, has addressed the powerful uplifting potential of doing meaningful work with a sense of purpose. He speaks of work that we really believe in and value because of the way it contributes to our own and others' lives.

> To have a firm persuasion in our work—to feel that what we do is right for ourselves and good for the world at the exactly same time—is one of the great triumphs of human existence. We do feel, when we have work that is challenging and enlarging and that seems to be doing something for others, as if . . . we could move mountains, as if we could call the world home; and for a while, in our imaginations, no matter the small size of our apartment, we dwell in a spacious house with endless horizons."[98]

Ben Cohen and Jerry Greenfield are good examples of how the power of purpose can help shape a successful career and rewarding life. They started their famous Ben & Jerry's ice cream company after early career failures—Ben to become a potter and Jerry to get into medical school. They both loved food, so they decided to create a profitable business married to a social purpose for pursuing this interest. Through their business they made a commitment to "Be the best ice cream company in the world . . . be viewed as master ice cream makers . . . (to give) customers what they want, when they want it, every single time."[99]

In terms of benefiting society and the world, they built directly into their mission statement a commitment to "Support nonviolent ways to resolve conflict . . . create economic opportunities for the disenfranchised . . . practicing caring capitalism . . . the environment . . . family farming . . ."[100]

Ben and Jerry combined passionate interests in food with being socially conscious. In doing so they created a successful business founded on a solid purpose of serving not only their customers but the world at large. Ben and Jerry have set a striking example of creating a sense of purpose as a crucial emotional discipline choice that can help in reaching positive dreams. The challenge for each of us is to discover our own sense of purpose.

For many, at the heart of a search for purpose is discovering what is frequently referred to as their "calling." During a recent trip to St. Petersburg, Russia, my wife and I visited the famous Hermitage Museum. While we were there we were informed that the mostly artistic (and often priceless) holdings were so vast that if a person were to spend a mere minute looking at each piece of art it would take eight years to see everything in the museum. We were struck by the immense beauty and value of the art by famous artists such as Van Gogh, Rembrandt, and Da Vinci while so many people on the streets outside the museum walls were struggling to simply make ends meet in St. Petersburg's suffering economy.

So why so much art when there is a great need for seemingly more practical effort to help meet the harsher realities of life such as the need for food and shelter? The answer, we simply concluded, is that is what artists do, create art. It's their calling and provides their sense of purpose in life, not to mention the inspiration that beautiful art brings to others, perhaps especially when their lives are mostly filled with continuous efforts to simply survive.

Abraham Maslow put it this way,

> A musician must make music, an artist must paint, a poet must write, if he is to be at peace with himself. What a man must be, he must be.[101]

In his book *Let Your Life Speak* author Parker Palmer addressed the issue of our vocation as a key source of a purposeful life. He especially emphasized the importance of listening within (a good strategy, by the way, to combine with "the power of silence," the focus of Chapter 20). He put it this way:

> I must listen to my life and try to understand what it is truly about . . . . That insight is hidden in the word vocation itself, which is rooted in the Latin word "voice."

Vocation does not mean a goal that I pursue. It means a calling that I hear. Before I can tell my life what I want to do with it, I must listen to my life telling me who I am. I must listen for the truths and values at the heart of my own identity, not the standards by which I must live—but the standards by which I cannot help but live if I am living my own life.[102]

This kind of deep inner listening is a form of profound emotional discipline. It requires patience and a process of letting go. At its most basic level it requires a transcending of the ego. Palmer had more to add to this insight:

Behind this understanding of vocation is a truth that the ego does not want to hear because it threatens the ego's turf . . . this is what the poet knows and what every wisdom tradition teaches: there is a great gulf between the way my ego wants to identify me, with its protective masks and self-serving fictions, and my true self.[103]

Ultimately, choosing to discover a personal purpose can help us to find authenticity in our lives. Aligning our work and life pursuits with our unique nature can introduce authenticity into our experiences. And living authentically, with a sense of purpose, can be a primary source of emotional stability and inner peace. It can free us from the turmoil of being tossed in swirling winds of fluctuating mental and emotional forces. Nineteenth-century English author James Allen put it well in his book *As a Man Thinketh:*

Thought allied fearlessly to purpose becomes creative force: he who knows this is ready to become something higher and stronger than a mere bundle of wavering thoughts and fluctuating sensations; he who does this has become the conscious and intelligent wielder of his mental powers.[104]

Choice 23

Have an Out-of-Ego Experience

~~~~~

He who is full of himself,
is likely to be quite empty.[105]

An article on the scandal at Enron Corporation looked beyond the dark story of upper management's abuse of power and how the executives misrepresented the organization's financial situation, leading to bankruptcy and the loss of the life savings of thousands of workers. Instead, it examined what motivated Enron workers to want to work there and provided important clues about how such mass deception could be accomplished.[106] It revealed a story of how the human condition can make us vulnerable to the allure of gaining importance, opportunity, and riches. Ultimately it revealed a story of the power of the ego.

The emotion-filled comments of former Enron employees were quite revealing. One said, "The opportunity... lit me on fire. It was like a drug." Another commented, "The risk was not going to Enron and not having the chance to fulfill my aspirations." Still another said, "For an energy-efficiency nut... Enron was like nirvana."[107] Working for Enron carried with it a strong emotional appeal for many workers who saw the company as a chance for not only a better life but an opportunity to fulfill their dreams. Perhaps this sad story leads to the recurrent conclusion of many philosophers, psychologists, and spiritual teachers alike. That is, our ultimate struggle in finding a healthy and fulfilling life resides within ourselves. And the most formidable challenger of all is that inner force generally referred to as the ego.

The ego resides within, but it can powerfully shape how we see things outside. It can in fact shape our very world. Most of us live in a world filled with ego. It is natural to view aspects of life in terms of how they affect us. But if we allow this tendency to mindlessly unfold, it can lead to some rather unfortunate views about our life experience. If the meeting room we are in, along with many other people, becomes warm and stuffy, it can seem like a personal inconvenience directed at us specifically. When a baby begins to cry during the climax of a captivating movie playing in a full theatre, it can feel as if only we are bothered.

Similarly, when praise and recognition are being doled out to members of a group or organization we belong to, the praise we receive personally seems to matter most. If criticism is being served up, the primary negative feelings we experience stem from whatever negative evaluation seems to be directed at us specifically. And we look to see if we get our fair share of benefits, rewards, inheritance, and even the fresh baked pie being served for dessert. So it goes—much of the time, if left unchecked, the ego rules.

The "ego" is a handy catch-all concept for the source of not only our strongest human wants and desires but also our disappointments, anger, indignation, frustration, and the bulk of our other negative feelings in life. "It's not fair!" "How dare she say that to me!" "I don't deserve this garbage!" "Why does this stuff always happen to me?!" When the ego gets ruffled, life can feel pretty bad indeed.

Frequently, the key to turning things around is not so much to change what is going on in our lives but to get "out of the ego." One arena where this is particularly important is interpersonal relationships, especially when there is a disagreement. Joel and Kate Feldman, directors of the Conscious Relationship Institute, teach a powerful communication-mirroring technique they call the

"Conscious Dialogue."[108] Although challenging to master, and containing several nuances best learned through repeated practice, a quick summary of the technique follows. When you feel your emotions arising in response to criticism or frustration expressed by someone toward you, make a disciplined choice to:

~ Mirror back what you hear being said without making a judgment or trying to interpret hidden meanings

~ Ask if you are understanding correctly and if there is more that the other person wants to say

~ And finally express what you can understand in what the person is saying and affirm their feelings

I have both experienced and observed in others the power of this technique for breaking loose from the ego and processing difficult emotional moments constructively. At a practical level it can accomplish the kind of out-of-ego listening that is expressed in the poignant words of psychology professor and author Michael P. Nichols,

> Genuine listening means suspending memory, desire and judgment—and, for a moment at least, existing for the other person.[109]

If we can shake loose of the grip of our insatiable egos, we can experience life from a fresh new perspective.

Poetry is yet another tool that can help us separate from our usual ego-based perceptions. Both writing and reading poetry can unleash a more transcendent view of the world. Consider the following poem.

Perfect Imperfections
Up the road most traveled by
I met my potent inner lie.
Amongst the beauty in my life
I found light storms of inner strife.
Every perfect hill or cloud
was a gift in darkened shroud.
Peaceful gratitude escaped my hold
because my ego was much too bold.
For every hallowed well shaped tree
I thought of more pleasing far from me.
In the blue and sacred sky
I recalled more glorious in mind's eye.
Crystal rain drops began to fall
but not as perfect as my recall.
I knew then why peace eludes my touch,
I miss the splendor in way too much.
In a person, plant, or brook
potential joy escapes my look.
The closer I see the pieces of my life
I bleed from imperfection's cutting knife.
Nothing, nothing can withstand
the critical scrutiny I command.
And so the sights on distant shore
seem more precious to explore.
Yet the real beauty is at hand
in my life right where I stand.
To look more deeply at the flaws
and see in them a heavenly cause.
And only then to find the bliss,

bestowed on each a sacred kiss.
Each living piece of puzzle grand
was shaped and fashioned by God's hand.
To see vast oceans in one drop of dew
and behold the heavens in a breath I blew.
To sense all creatures in one tiny flea
and God's own face in all I see.
Such imperfections perfect be,
It's now God's eye from which I see.

—Charles C. Manz

There is yet another approach for choosing to have an out-of ego experience. Chapter 9 outlined some basic techniques for meditation. By combining meditation with the popular phrase "Let go and let God," we can create a very effective strategy. After relaxing the body, and as deep abdominal breathing is being established, simply repeat in the mind "let go" on the out breath and "let God" (or "let Godliness" or "let universal energy" or some other phrase that works for you) on the in breath. Each time "let go" is repeated, picture all the negative emotion, ego involvement with the world, and even any sense of who you are, flowing out of the body (sometimes it helps to picture these things flowing out as dark smoke). And as "let God" (or "let Godliness" . . .) is repeated on the in breath, picture healing light entering the body and the power of the universe redirecting your life in positive and powerful ways.

It is not necessary to meditate (although it can be quite helpful to most people) to benefit from this approach. Simply choose to have an out-of-ego experience regularly. Periodically throughout the day, especially when you find your ego taking hold of your outlook and negative feelings invading your life, momentarily stop what you are doing. Picture yourself letting go of your thoughts, your feelings . . . your ego. Then picture positive universal, even spiritual, energy taking over and redirecting your current responses. Let go and let Godliness. It is a powerful life-changing strategy that you can choose to help you "feel good" and to more fully experience your life in all its wonder.

Choice 24

What About Love?

~~~~~

The day will come when, after harnessing space,
the winds, the tides, and gravitation,
we shall harness for God the energies of love.
And on that day, for the second time
in the history of the world,
we shall have discovered fire.

—Pierre Teilhard de Chardin

Love is the dimension of existence that can elevate us to our very best and leave us most vulnerable to all life has to offer, both the wonderful and the painful. Love has tremendous transformational power. It is a potent ingredient for how we feel about life. When we choose to love, we can make ourselves vulnerable to being hurt but we also open ourselves to probably the most positive feelings in life. Love can elevate even the very worst of circumstances.

During an interview President George W. Bush commented on the importance of love, especially from his parents, for enabling him to live a full and successful life with relatively little worry. "I love my parents . . . they gave me unconditional love. They said, 'Son, we love you whether you succeed or fail.' Unconditional love is liberating, and it gave me the chance to dare to succeed. Because of it, I'm a risk-taker. Obviously, I wouldn't be sitting here in the White House had I not taken the risk of running for the presidency. People say to me, 'Aren't you worried about failing?' The answer is no, because deep down inside I know that the core of me is based upon the greatest gift one can have, which is unconditional love."[110]

Imagine that—sincerely feeling that you are loved no matter whether you succeed or fail. In the context of unconditional love, much of the worry and negative feeling in life simply evaporate.

One of the most moving descriptions of love is contained in the New Testament in a letter written by Paul to the Corinthians. The letter suggests that we will not really live and experience life, no matter how outwardly successful we seem, if we lack love. And when we know how to truly love, everything in our lives is transformed—we will enjoy the ultimate positive and healthy feelings that life has to offer. The following are excerpts from this passage:

> ... if I have prophetic powers, and understand all mysteries and all knowledge, and if I have all faith, so as to remove mountains, but do not have love, I am nothing ...
>
> Love is patient; love is kind; love is not rude. It does not insist on its own way; it is not irritable or resentful; it does not rejoice in wrongdoing, but rejoices in the truth. It bears all things, believes all things, hopes all things, endures all things.
>
> Love never ends ... faith, hope, and love abide, these three; and the greatest of these is love. (1 Corinthians 13, 2-13, New Revised Standard Version)

Many believe this is the most beautiful description of love ever written. It has been a favorite for inclusion in wedding ceremonies because it is a glimpse at what love could be at its best. Maybe it is the kind of love President Bush was talking about. Unfortunately, love has also been badly mislabeled, misunderstood, and misused.

The pursuit of love, whether in the form of a romantic relationship or true caring and compassion received from family and friends, has caused many to attempt to grasp and manipulate for what must be freely given as a gift. Every time we encounter painful conflict, hurtfulness, loneliness, or any number of other difficult aspects of relationship, the ultimate transformative power is love. But most of us barely begin to understand it, if at all.

I don't claim to have any magical answers to the mystery of how we can allow love to transform even the deepest sense of emptiness or despair in our lives, but I believe it can. Yet it's far too much of a mystery to expect that we can take hold of it like some mysterious power tool to make our entire lives a magical feel-good experience that transcends our limited images of what is possible. But I do believe that it can vastly elevate our whole existence if we allow love to find fertile soil to grow, as it will, in us. We can start by opening to the possibility of love in our lives, in all its wondrous forms. Then by taking even small steps to extend caring and compassion toward others—saying a kind word, lending a helping hand, and just being there for someone in need—we may well find that we have made a choice to enjoy some of the most powerful and positive feelings life has to offer.

And love need not be restricted to our personal lives. Dorothy Marcic, author of the book *Managing with the Wisdom of Love*, points out that while the curriculum for MBA and management training programs has not traditionally addressed the importance of loving co-workers or clients, she makes it clear that such training could be a key ingredient for building healthier and more spiritual organizations:

> What would it mean if we would love our subordinates, our bosses, our colleagues, and ourselves? It would mean we would not intentionally hurt them, we wouldn't treat them unjustly, and we would act towards them with dignity and respect. Such are the building blocks of a healthy and thriving system . . . if

you treat all the people you work with the way you would like to be treated, then you are in fact operating through the wisdom of love. And if all the executives and managers of the organization are guided by this principle in the decisions they make, then we can say that the organization, the cumulative entity, has spirituality as at least part of its foundation.[111]

Marcic provides us with a glimpse of a different kind of world where, despite our rational "grown-up maturity," we are not ashamed to admit our need for something as basic and powerful as love. To close this chapter I will share some comments of small children on the subject of love that were included in an e-mail message that was circulated on the Internet. Sometimes wisdom is found in the seemingly most unlikely places. Consider love for a moment through the eyes of small children and see if it opens some new insights for you about this powerful force for uplifting your life and spirit. I hope that these words, as they did for me, will bring you good feelings, a smile, and a little wisdom about love.

Wisdom on Love as Viewed Through the Eyes of Small Children

Love is the first feeling you feel before all the bad stuff gets in the way.—Charlie, age 5

When my Grandmother got arthritis, she couldn't bend over and paint her toenails anymore. So my grandfather does it for her all the time, even when his hands got arthritis too. That's love.—Rebecca, age 8

Love is when someone hurts you. And you get so mad but you don't yell at them because you know it would hurt their feelings.—Samantha, age 6

Love is when you go out to eat and give somebody most of your French fries without making them give you any of theirs.—Chrissy, age 6

Love is what makes you smile when you're tired.—Teri, age 4

If you want to learn to love better, you should start with a friend who you hate.—Nikka, age 6

Love is what's in the room with you at Christmas if you stop opening presents and listen.—Bobby, age 5

You think when you tell someone something bad about yourself and you're scared, they won't love you anymore. But then you get surprised because they still love you, but even more.—Matthew, age 7

Love is when your puppy licks your face even after you left him alone all day.—Mary Ann, age 4

Choice 25

Get a Life, with Spirit

~~~~~

Life is what happens to us
while we are making other plans.[112]

—Thomas la Mance

*G*et a life" is a common expression, often spoken in a less than complimentary tone. The phrase is often used as an insult directed at someone who is seen to be focusing on trivial concerns.

~ ~ ~ ~ ~

"Can you believe the new department stationery that the division manager ordered? I don't think the letterhead is very attractive. Do you, Tom?"

"Given all the other problems we've got going on right now with recent sales decreases and the possibility of major layoffs in our division, how can you focus on something as trivial as stationery? Shoshana, you need to get a life!"

~ ~ ~ ~ ~

We can recognize the timeliness of this kind of challenge when we see others fixated on things that seem of little significance. In some ways, however, the various issues discussed in this book challenge all of us to "get a life!" Certainly, it is worth considering whether we have meaning and significance in our lives, but that is not the whole story. Perhaps it is not that we are spending our days wrestling with needless trivia that we shouldn't be wasting our time (and our lives) on. Rather, it may be that we are mostly just going through the motions, even if our work and our roles in life do have real significance.

It is too easy to become numbed to life and go from hour to hour and day to day in a kind of daze, with no sense of purpose, enthusiasm, or value placed on the gift of being alive. Who hasn't had the experience of driving or walking on a familiar route and reaching our destination only to realize we were barely aware of our surroundings, even on a gorgeous day? Similarly, our lives can become bogged down with our immediate frustrating or difficult circumstances and the feelings that they foster. We can go through entire days focusing on annoying details and miss all the opportunities to be thankfully alive.

Ultimately, if we sincerely think about these kinds of ideas, we will find ourselves confronted by an even more revealing challenge. We are challenged to think deeply about the way we are spending the time that we have in this world. We come face to face with probing questions such as "Do I *really* have a life?" "Do I have a life, *with spirit?*" and "what does it *really* mean to have a life *with spirit?*" To answer these kinds of questions in a way that can have significance for how we will live from now on, we may need to transcend our normal plane of existence and to see things anew from a very different perspective.

One method that I have found that shakes me from my habitual views and daily routines is to try viewing the world poetically (I shared a similar idea in Chapter 23 for having an out-of-ego experience). When I try to view even the most common situations from the standpoint of creating poetry, the world seems to significantly change in an instant, becoming more spirited and alive somehow. As an example of breaking long-established petrified views of common things in the world, consider the following poem. It provides an artistic glimpse of how the limiting views that can hold us back, and that cause our lives to become lifeless, can be transformed before our very eyes.

Soul Song

I looked down upon a star
and up upon the ground.
I looked clear through a cold brick wall
and at a sightless sound.

I ate a glass of full ripe wine
and drank a piece of pie.
A rope did shine upon the earth.
A moon beam I did tie.

I blew upon a scented rose
and sniffed some smooth white stones.
I slumbered to a loud shrill noise
and danced to silent tones.

I put some jewelry in my hair
and then my ears I curled.
I looked outside upon my heart
And deep inside the world.

I flew up through the clear blue sea
and washed with angels' hair.
I breathed water from a crystal stream
and swam upon the air.

At last I felt myself awake,
I'd been spirit dead so long.
Living thoughts brought my soul alive
and it burst into song.

—Charles C. Manz

The challenge for each of us is to find ways to be more alive in our living. If we can choose to see, hear, smell, taste, and touch the world in new ways, we can awaken the spirit within us. And in doing so we can create a fuller and more spirited life.

I wish you the very best as you continue on your own life journey. I sincerely hope that you will discover the powerful choices that you have about the way you feel and the significant impact they have on your life. I wish you an extraordinary life with spirit!

Other Spirit-Centered Emotional Discipline Choices

~*Attend a conference or retreat that includes the topic of spirituality.* For example, "spirituality in the workplace" has been the focus of many such events and has attracted the interest of many major organizations and executives from across the world.

~*Study spiritual traditions* including both religious and nonreligious perspectives. Becoming more familiar with the teachings and histories of prominent religious and spiritual views can be both interesting and enriching.

~*Seek out opportunities to serve.* Giving of yourself as you participate in worthwhile service of others who need your support can be rewarding and uplifting for both you and them.

~*Try practicing spiritual disciplines* such as those included in Richard Foster's classic book *Celebration of Discipline* (Harper San Francisco, 1998). The specific disciplines he reviews include meditation, prayer, fasting, study, solitude, and confession.

~*Visualize that you are sending out the energy of love and compassion* toward those whom you encounter.

Imagining that your positive energy is actually uplift-ing others can be an emotionally uplifting experience for yourself.

~ *Consciously look for the positive spirit in each person* (you might think of this as the spirit put there by God). Choose to look beyond the self-centered ego of others and instead focus on your awareness of their unique positive spirit within.

~ How might you adapt the above ideas to create emo-tional discipline strategies that you can apply in your life and work? What additional Emotional Discipline Choice ideas can you think of?

Learning how to combine the powerful forces of the mind, body, emotions, and spirit to choose how we feel is like growing inner wings for life. And feeling good is a choice we can make every day when we have such wings.

~~~~~~~~

Be like the bird that,
pausing in her flight awhile on boughs too slight,
feels them give way beneath her and yet sings,
knowing that she hath wings.

—Victor Hugo

The Power to Choose How You Feel Motto

~ ~ ~ ~ ~

We must not cease from exploration
and the end of all our exploring will be
to arrive where we began and
to know the place for the first time.

—T. S. Eliot

*E*arly in this book I shared many aspects of effective emotional discipline both for dealing with current challenging situations and for increasing your capacity for meeting future challenges. These included key requirements and decisions for making a commitment to its practice; fundamental characteristics, paradoxes, and limitations involved; and especially the central role of *choice* for gaining the power to choose how you feel.

I also described the key steps for creating a comprehensive process for practicing emotional discipline in response to emotionally challenging situations. Such a process is intended to be a central part of learning to more systematically practice emotional discipline in your life and at work. I pointed out that the process can and should be modified to fit your particular life circumstances. Although I described in detail a complete generic version of such a process in Chapter 1, for the sake of convenience, the process is summarized again in the box on the next page.

Most of the book addressed 25 specific choices that you can apply to positively affect the way you feel. While each of these is an alternative for enacting step 5 of the process (choosing an emotional discipline strategy), they can be selected and applied during any of the 5 steps as desired without having to work through the entire process. These strategies tap into the powerful forces of the mind, body, emotions, and spirit. When these tools are all brought together, they can help create a foundation for an uplifted life.

It is likely that you have found some of the strategies more helpful for your particular circumstances than others.

1. What is the *Cause*?

Identify the issue or event that is provoking the feelings.

2. Focus on Your *Body*

Scan your body. Determine the location of your physical sensations and whether they are uncomfortable or pleasant.

Rate your physical feelings on a scale ranging from −10 (very uncomfortable/painful) to +10 (very comfortable/enjoyable).

3. Focus on Your *Mind*

Identify your thoughts (internal statements and/or mental pictures) that accompany the feelings.

Identify your beliefs that underlie your thoughts that are laying the foundation for your mental and physical reactions.

4. Focus on Your *Spirit*

Determine what part of yourself is being revealed and what part is being hidden. Learn more about the different aspects of yourself that you live from and a sense of which you would like to have more revealed and which you would not.

5. Make a *Choice*

Choose an emotional discipline strategy and apply it to gain in power to choose how you feel.

I hope you will select the ones that are most relevant for you and begin to apply them regularly in your life. You may have also thought of ways to modify some of the strategies or identified some different ones of your own (perhaps inspired by the ideas for additional choices suggested on pages 118, 160, and 206) that are better suited to the specific challenges that you face. This is a useful step and an important part of creating your own approach for embracing the powerful reality that you can choose how you feel.

Of course, the realities of everyday life, especially the trials and difficulties that life presents you with, can unleash challenging feelings and painful experiences. And difficult feelings will at times just come up without any apparent immediate external event that triggers them. Responding by trying to avoid and escape these feelings without really dealing with them, or by seeking quick fix "feel-good" choices that only temporarily cover them up, can be self-defeating. Rather than ignoring, fleeing from, or postponing facing the way we feel, we need to constructively work with the primary forces of mind, body, emotions, and spirit in our lives.

To begin meeting the challenge of choosing to feel better and be better from this day forward, an important step is to make a crucial mental shift that embraces the power you possess for positively practicing emotional discipline in your life. To help move this process along I have one last tool to share that is designed to help you get started in applying the techniques in this book. Specifically, it consists of learning and incorporating into your daily living what I call "The Power to Choose How You Feel Motto." Again, you are invited to adapt this motto to your specific needs if that is something that you would like to do. Or perhaps you will find the way it is currently written seems just fine for helping you get started on your journey toward learning to choose how you feel every day.

Consider carefully the Motto on the following page. You can copy it and carry it with you in your purse or wallet or even commit it to memory. Let it sink deeply into your thinking and try to begin living in a way that is consistent with its basic principles. Let it produce a lasting profound life change. Commit to having a choice about how you feel from this day forward.

The
Power to Choose How You Feel
Motto

~ ~ ~

My feelings are a natural part of life that affect all of my
experiences. If I feel bad my life can seem pretty bleak,
and if I feel good my whole world can seem to become a
better place. The good news is that the way I feel is a
choice I can make every day. By collaborating with the
natural forces available in my mind, body, emotions,
and spirit, I can create a positive lens through which
I experience life. I truly can uplift my life and spirit
when I fully embrace and constructively act upon
the reality that I have

The Power to Choose How I Feel.

Notes

~ ~ ~ ~ ~

[1] See the article "Emotional Intelligence," by P. Salovey and J. D. Mayer, *Imagination, Cognition, and Personality*, Vol. 9, 1990, p.186.

[2] See the book *The Heart of the Soul: Emotional Awareness* by Gary Zukav and Linda Francis (New York: Simon & Schuster, 2001).

[3] See the book *Practicing the Power of Now*, by Eckhart Tolle (Novato, CA: New World Library, 2001), p. 24.

[4] *Hooked on Feeling Bad: 3 Steps to Living a Life You Love!* by Joyce Moskowitz (Davie, FL: Clear Vision Publishing, 2000) p. 122.

[5] See the book *Celebration of Discipline: The Path to Spiritual Growth* by Richard J. Foster (San Francisco: HarperSanFrancisco, 1998) p. 2.

[6] See the article "Emotional Capability, Emotional Intelligence, and Radical Change," by Quy Nguyen Huy, *Academy of Management Review*, Vol. 24, 1999, pp. 325–345.

[7] See the article "Progress on a Cognitive-Motivational-Relational Theory of Emotion" by R. S. Lazarus, *American Psychologist*, Vol. 46, 1991, pp. 819–834 (quote is on p. 820).

[8] For more information on this area of research, see the article "Emotion Regulation: Affective, Cognitive, and Social Consequences" by James J. Gross, *Psychophysiology*, Vol. 39, 2002, pp. 281–291.

[9] Ibid., p. 282.

[10] Ibid., p. 282; and J. J. Gross, "The Emerging Field of Emotion Regulation: An Integrative Review," *Review of General Psychology*, Vol. 2, 1998, pp. 271–299.

[11] See A. M. Isen, "The Influence of Positive and Negative Affect on Cognitive Organization: Some Implications for Development," in N. Stein, B. Leventhal and J. Trabasso (eds.), *Psychology and Biological Approaches to Emotion* (Hillsdale, NJ: Lawrence, Erlbaum Associates, 1990), pp. 75–94; and A. M. Isen, K. A. Daubman, and G. P. Nowicki, "Positive Affect Facilitates Creative Problem Solving." *Journal of Personality and Social Psychology*, Vol. 52, 1987, pp. 1122–1131.

[12] Edward Vela, "Emotion in the Classroom," *Teaching Excellence*, Vol. 12, 2000–2001, pp. 1–2.

¹³This quote is taken from *Phillips Book of Great Thoughts & Funny Sayings* by Bob Phillips (Wheaton, IL: Tyndale House Publishers, 1993), p. 110.

¹⁴"The Autobiography of Charles Darwin" from *The Life and Letters of Charles Darwin*, edited by Francis Darwin (various editions available).

¹⁵For a comprehensive description of self-leadership and how it can be applied to enhance personal effectiveness, see *Mastering Self-Leadership: Empowering Yourself for Personal Excellence*, 2nd ed. by Charles C. Manz and Christopher P. Neck (Upper Saddle River, NJ: Prentice Hall, 1999).

¹⁶This quote is from the book *The Wisdom of Menopause: Creating Physical and Emotional Health and Healing During the Change* by Christiane Northrup (New York: Bantam Books, 2001), p. 57.

¹⁷Both of these quotes are taken from the online article "Sports Guru Phil" by Mark Rowland, *Los Angeles Magazine*, June 2000, pp.1–7 (p. 2).

¹⁸For more insight regarding Phil Jackson's unorthodox, even spiritual, coaching methods see the book *Sacred Hoops* by Phil Jackson and Hugh Delehanty (New York: Hyperion, 1995).

¹⁹See the article "Emotion Regulation: Affective, Cognitive, and Social Consequences" by James J. Gross, *Psychophysiology*, Vol. 39, 2002, pp. 281–291.

²⁰See the article "Emotion in the Workplace: The New Challenge for Managers" by Neal M. Ashkanasy and Catherine S. Daus, *Academy of Management Executive*, Vol. 16, 2002, pp. 76–86.

²¹For more information on this study, see the article "'Short' Gene Linked to Fear" (originally published in the *Los Angeles Times*), *Daily Hampshire Gazette* (North Hampton, MA), July 19, 2002, Vol. 216, pp. A1, A7.

²²This quote is taken from *Phillips Book of Great Thoughts & Funny Sayings* by Bob Phillips (Wheaton, IL: Tyndale House Publishers, 1993), p. 317.

²³See the article "How the Bust Saved Silicon Valley . . . Silicon Valley Reboots," *Newsweek*, March 25, 2002, p. 42.

²⁴Viktor E. Frankl, *Man's Search for Meaning* (New York: Simon & Schuster, 1984).

²⁵See Daniel Goleman, *Emotional Intelligence*, (New York: Bantam, 1995).

²⁶See the book *Working with Emotional Intelligence* by Daniel Goleman (New York: Bantam, 1998), p. 317.

²⁷See the article "Emotional Intelligence as a Moderator of Emotional and Behavioral Reactions to Job Insecurity" by Peter J. Jordan, Neal M. Ashkanasy, and Charmine E. J. Hartel, *Academy of Management Review*, Vol. 27, 2002, pp. 361–372.

²⁸Daniel Goleman, Richard Boyatzis, and Annie McKee, *Primal Leadership: Realizing the Power of Emotional Intelligence* (Boston: Massachusetts: Harvard Business School Press, 2002).

[29]See the article "Four Pillars of Excellence" by Steve Ballmer, *Executive Excellence*, Vol. 19, April 2002, pp. 3–4.

[30]This quote is from the book *Beating the Street* by Peter Lynch with John Rothchild (New York: Simon & Schuster, 1993), p. 36.

[31]This quote is taken from *Phillips Book of Great Thoughts & Funny Sayings* by Bob Phillips (Wheaton, IL: Tyndale House Publishers, 1993), p. 302.

[32]Jon Kabat-Zinn, *Wherever You Go, There You Are* (New York: Hyperion, 1994).

[33]This quote is from the book *The Tao of Leadership*, a translation of Lao Tzu's *Tao Te Ching* by John Heider (New York: Bantam, 1986) p. 135.

[34]Ibid., p. 137.

[35]For more on effective ways to turn external attacks into helpful energy, see the book *Getting to Yes* 2nd ed., by Roger Fisher and William Ury (New York: Penguin Books, 1991).

[36]See the essay by Martin Rutte, "Spirituality in the Workplace," included in the book *Heart at Work* edited by Jack Canfield and Jacqueline Miller (New York, McGraw-Hill, 1996), p. 247.

[37]This quote is taken from the book *Quotable Women: A Collection of Shared Thoughts* (Philadelphia, PA: Running Press, 1994).

[38]These excerpts are taken from the book *You Can Be Happy No Matter What* by Richard Carlson (Novato, CA: New World Library, 1997), pp. 121–129.

[39]For more about what the Dalai Lama has to say about happiness and the choices that we make that cause us unhappiness, see the book *The Art of Happiness: A Handbook for Living* by the Dalai Lama and Howard C. Cutler (New York: Riverhead Books, 1998). The specific quotes used in this passage appear on page 151.

[40]See the book *Wherever You Go, There You Are: Mindfulness Meditation in Everyday Life* by Jon Kabat-Zinn (New York: Hyperion, 1994), p. 4.

[41]Richard Carlson, *Don't Sweat the Small Stuff . . . and It's All Small Stuff* (New York: Hyperion, 1997), p.173.

[42]This quote is taken from the book *Quotable Women: A Collection of Shared Thoughts* (Philadelphia, PA: Running Press, 1994).

[43]See the essay by Bill Gates "New Rules for the Age of Information" contained in the book *The Little Book of Business Wisdom*, edited by Peter Krass (New York: Wiley, 2001), pp. 8–11.

[44]This information is based in part on the booklet *A Pocket Guide to NLP* (Niles, IL: Nightengale–Conant Corporation, 1991) that accompanies the audiotape-based learning program titled *NLP: The New Technology of Achievement*, p. 6.

[45]For some detailed home training containing more information and techniques for practicing NLP, you may want to consider the Nightengale-Conant distrib-

uted audiotape programs titled *NLP: The New Technology of Achievement*, (1991) and *Success Mastery with NLP* (1992).

[46]This quote is taken from *Phillips Book of Great Thoughts & Funny Sayings* by Bob Phillips (Wheaton, IL: Tyndale House Publishers, 1993), p. 310.

[47]Norman Vincent Peale, *The Power of Positive Thinking*, Centennial Edition (Englewood Cliffs, NJ: Prentice Hall, 1952, 1978), p. 86.

[48]See, for example, the new book by Martin Seligman *Authentic Happiness: Using the New Positive Psychology to Realize Your Potential for Lasting Fulfillment* (New York: Free Press, 2003).

[49]See, for example, the article "Positive Organizational Behavior: Developing and Managing Psychological Strengths for Performance Improvement" by Fred Luthans, *Academy of Management Executive*, forthcoming 2002, and the book *Positive Organizational Scholarship* by Kim S. Cameron, Jane E. Dutton and Robert E. Quinn (San Francisco: Berrett-Koehler, forthcoming 2003).

[50]Martin E. P. Seligman, *Learned Optimism* (New York: Alfred A. Knopf, 1991), p. 16.

[51]Norman Vincent Peale, *The Power of Positive Thinking*, Centennial Edition (Englewood Cliffs, NJ: Prentice Hall, 1952, 1978), p. 86.

[52]Fred Fengler and Todd Varnum, *Manifesting Your Heart's Desire* (Burlington, VT: HeartLight Publishing, 1994, 2000).

[53]See the book *Psycho-Cybernetics* by Maxwell Maltz (Englewood Cliffs, NJ: Prentice Hall, 1960) and the newer release *The New Psycho-Cybernetics* by Maxwell Maltz and Dan S. Kennedy (Englewood Cliffs, NJ: Prentice Hall, 2002).

[54]*The Art of Happiness: A Handbook for Living* by His Holiness the Dalai Lama and Howard C. Cutler (New York: Riverhead Books, 1998), pp. 68–69.

[55]For more information on a very similar technique, see the book *Feeling Good: The New Mood Therapy* (especially chapters 4, 5 and 6) by David D. Burns (New York: Avon Books, 1999).

[56]This quote is taken from *Phillips Book of Great Thoughts & Funny Sayings* by Bob Phillips (Wheaton, IL: Tyndale House Publishers, 1993), p.156.

[57]This quote is taken from the book *Wherever You Go, There You Are* by Jon Kabat-Zinn (New York: Hyperion, 1994), p. 18.

[58]*The Medical Advisor: The Complete Guide to Alternative and Conventional Treatments*, by the Editors of Time-Life Books (Alexandria, VA: Time-Life, 1997).

[59]See especially pages 203–207 of the book by Andrew Weil, *Spontaneous Healing: How to Discover and Enhance Your Body's Natural Ability to Maintain and Heal Itself* (New York: Fawcett Columbine Books, 1995).

[60]See the article "Bush Pushes Fitness Message," by Lawrence L. Knutson, *Boston Globe*, June 23, 2002, p. A16.

[61]See the section titled "Health & Medicine: Don't Just Sit There" in the May 1, 2000 issue of the *Wall Street Journal*, pp R1–R20.

[62]For more information on executives' fitness, see the articles "Fit to Lead: Is Fitness the Key to Effective Executive Leadership?" by Christopher P. Neck, T. L. Mitchell, Charles C. Manz, Kenneth H. Cooper, and Emmet C. Thompson, II, *Journal of Managerial Psychology*, Vol. 15, 2000, pp. 833–840; and "The Fit Executive: Exercise and Diet Guidelines for Enhanced Performance," by Christopher P. Neck and Kenneth H. Cooper, *Academy of Management Executive*, Vol. 14, 2000, pp. 72–83.

[63]Andrew Weil, *Spontaneous Healing: How to Discover and Enhance Your Body's Natural Ability to Maintain and Heal Itself* (New York: Fawcett Columbine Books, 1995), p. 187.

[64]For detailed information on the relation between how we feel and food and advice on how to effectively manage this process, see the book *Food & Mood: The Complete Guide to Eating Well and Feeling Your Best*, 2nd ed. by Elizabeth Somer (New York: Owl Books, 1999).

[65]See the article "HealthSmart" by Tedd Mitchell, M.D., *USA Today Weekend*, December 29–31, 2000, p. 4. For more specifics and strategies for healthy eating, see Dr. Mitchell's column "Eat your Way to Better Heath," published January 21–23, 2000, p. 4, and for more specific strategies on exercise and fitness, see his article "Renew Your Fitness Vows," published March 10–11, 2000, p. 4.

[66]See the article "Resolve to be 'Good' 80% of the Time" by Tedd Mitchell, M.D., *USA Today Weekend*, December 31, 1999–January 2, 2000, p. 4.

[67]These quotes are taken from *Phillips Book of Great Thoughts & Funny Sayings* by Bob Phillips (Wheaton, IL: Tyndale House Publishers, 1993), pp. 223 and 163.

[68]*The Mozart Effect: Tapping the Power of Music to Heal the Body, Strengthen the Mind, and Unlock the Creative Spirit* by Don Campbell (New York: Quill, 2001).

[69]The audiotape program *Optimal Health* by Jim Loehr, Nick Hall, and Jack Groppel (Niles, IL: Nightengale-Conant, 1996).

[70]Norman Cousins, *Head First: The Biology of Hope and the Healing Power of the Human Spirit*, (New York: Penguin, 1990).

[71]C. W. Metcalf, *Lighten Up!: The Amazing Power of Grace Under Pressure* (Niles, IL: Nightengale-Conant, 1994).

[72]This passage is taken from the chapter "Sam Walton: Sam's Rules for Building a Business" in the book *The Little Book of Business Wisdom: Rules of Success from More Than 50 Business Legends*, edited by Peter Krass (New York: Wiley & Sons, 2001) p. 124.

[73]*The Medical Advisor: The Complete Guide to Alternative and Conventional Treatments*, by the Editors of Time-Life Books (Alexandria, VA: Time-Life, 1997), p. 21.

[74]Ibid., p. 20.

[75]For example, in the audio program *Mentally Fit Forever: How to Boost Brain Power at Any Age* (Niles, IL: Nightengale-Conant, 1999), Lee Pulos suggests a nine-step technique on tape side 3 of the program and on pages 12–13 of the accompanying booklet that he claims almost completely eliminates stress. It involves tapping certain points around the eyes and under the nose and mouth, and then next to the sternum and on the hand.

[76]This technique is recommended in *The Medical Advisor: The Complete Guide to Alternative and Conventional Treatments*, by the Editors of Time-Life Books (Alexandria, VA: Time-Life, 1997), p. 137.

[77]This quote is from the book *The Tao of Tai-Chi Chuan: Way to Rejuvenation* by Jou, Tsung Hwa and edited by Shoshana Shapiro (Warwick, New York: The Tai-Chi Foundation, 1991), pp. A15–16.

[78]For a good introduction to qigong, see the book *QiGong for Beginners* by Stanley D. Wilson (New York: Sterling Publishing Co., 1997). Another book on the subject is *Secrets of QiGong* by Angus Clark (DK Pub Merchandise, 2001).

[79]*The Complete Idiot's Guide to Tai Chi and QiGong* by Bill Douglas (Indianapolis, IN: Alpha Books, 1999), p. 4.

[80]For more information on tai chi, many books are available, including *The Complete Idiot's Guide to Tai Chi and QiGong* by Bill Douglas (Indianapolis, IN: Alpha Books, 1999) and *The Tao of Tai-Chi Chuan: Way to Rejuvenation* by Jou, Tsung Hwa and edited by Shoshana Shapiro (Warwick, New York: The Tai-Chi Foundation, 1991).

[81]*QiGong for Beginners* by Stanley D. Wilson (New York: Sterling Publishing Co., 1997).

[82]This passage is adapted from material in the book *Mastering Self-Leadership: Empowering Yourself for Personal Excellence*, 2nd ed. by Charles C. Manz and Christopher P. Neck (Upper Saddle River, NJ: Prentice Hall, 1999), p. 51.

[83]See the book *Finding Flow: The Psychology of Engagement with Everyday Life* by Mihaly Csikszentmihalyi (New York: Basic Books, 1997), pp. 46–47.

[84]*Flow: The Psychology of Optimal Experience* by Mihaly Csikszentmihalyi (New York: Harper Perennial, 1990), p. 6.

[85]Ibid., p. 105.

[86]*Finding Flow: The Psychology of Engagement with Everyday Life* by Mihaly Csikszentmihalyi (New York: Basic Books, 1997), p. 117.

[87]For a more detailed discussion on the idea of timelessness and its relation to creativity, see the article "When the Muse Takes it All: A Model for the Experience of Timelessness in Organizations," by Charalampos Mainemelis, *Academy of Management Review*, Vol. 26, 2001, pp. 548–565.

[88]This quote is published in the essay "Spirituality in the Workplace" by Martin Rutte, included in the book *Heart at Work* edited by Jack Canfield and Jacqueline Miller (New York, McGraw-Hill, 1996), p. 247.

[89]See the essay "On Living a Lie" by Richard Brodie, included in the book *Heart at Work* edited by Jack Canfield and Jacqueline Miller (New York: McGraw-Hill, 1996), pp. 20–24).

[90]This quote is taken from *Phillips Book of Great Thoughts & Funny Sayings* by Bob Phillips (Wheaton, IL: Tyndale House Publishers, 1993), p. 297.

[91]This quote is taken from *Phillips Book of Great Thoughts & Funny Sayings* by Bob Phillips (Wheaton, IL: Tyndale House Publishers, 1993), p. 288.

[92]*Getting to Yes*, 2nd Edition, by Roger Fisher and William Ury (New York: Penguin Books, 1991), p. 112.

[93]Parker J. Palmer, *Let Your Life Speak: Listening For the Voice of Vocation* (San Francisco: Jossey-Bass, 2000), pp. 5–6.

[94]This quote is taken from the book *Quotable Women: A Collection of Shared Thoughts.* (Philadelphia, PA: Running Press, 1994).

[95]This quote is from the classic book *Man's Search for Meaning* by Victor Frankl (New York: Washington Square Press, 1984), p. 165.

[96]Richard Leider, *The Power of Purpose: Creating Meaning in Your Life and Work* (San Francisco: Berrett-Koehler Publishers, 1997), p. 1.

[97]For more information on the idea of "altruistic egoism," see the classic book by Hans Selye *Stress Without Distress* (New York: Signet Books, 1974).

[98]From the book *Crossing the Unknown Sea: Work as a Pilgrimage of Identity*, by David Whyte (New York: Riverhead Books, 2001), p. 4.

[99]This material is taken from the chapter "Ben Cohen and Jerry Greenfield: Our Aspirations" in the book *The Little Book of Business Wisdom: Rules of Success from More Than 50 Business Legends*, edited by Peter Krass, (New York: Wiley & Sons, 2001), p. 172.

[100]Ibid., p.175.

[101]This quote is included in the book *The Book of Positive Quotations*, compiled and arranged by John Cook (New York: Gramercy Books, 1999 edition), p. 333.

[102]Parker J. Palmer, *Let Your Life Speak: Listening for the Voice of Vocation* (San Francisco: Jossey-Bass, 2000), pp. 4–5.

[103]Ibid., p. 5.

[104]James Allen, *As a Man Thinketh* (Philadelphia, PA: Running Press, 1989). The original book was written in the 19th century.

[105]This quote is taken from *Phillips Book of Great Thoughts & Funny Sayings* by Bob Phillips (Wheaton, IL: Tyndale House Publishers, 1993), p. 109.

[106]See the article "What If You Worked at Enron?" by Charles Fishman, *Fast Company*, May 2002, pp. 102–112.

[107]Ibid., p. 104.

[108]Joel and Kate Feldman conduct relationship workshops and retreats at the Kripalu Center for Yoga and Health, Box 793, Lenox, MA 01240-0793, www.kripalu.org .

[109]This quote was included in the "Leadership Thought of the Week" in the weekly e-mail of Adventure Quest-USA. The web site for Adventure Quest is www.AdventureQuest-USA.com.

[110]See the article "I'm Not Afraid to Seize the Moment" by Dotson Rader, *Parade Magazine*, April 29, 2001, pp. 4–6.

[111]Dorothy Marcic, *Managing with the Wisdom of Love: Uncovering Virtue in People and Organizations* (San Francisco: Jossey-Bass, 1997), p. 15.

[112]This quote is taken from *Phillips Book of Great Thoughts & Funny Sayings* by Bob Phillips (Wheaton, IL: Tyndale House Publishers, 1993), p. 195.

Index

~~~~~

disorder, Seasonal Affective
(SAD), 45
dissatisfaction, personal, 86–87
drama, subtelty, 172

Edison, Thomas, invention
process, 96–97
effect, The Mozart, 137
ego
out of, 187–194
vs. spirit, 25
egoism, altruistic, 181
Einstein, Albert
miracle perspective, 111
problem solving, 105
elements, effective manifestation,
114
elevators, vs. stairs, 161
Eliot, T.S., exploration, 209
emotion
blinded by, 1–2
defined, 5–6
emotional discipline
choices, 13–14
defined, 7–8
promise, 8–12
*Emotional Intelligence: Why It Can
Matter More Than IQ*
(Goleman), 62
Emotional Intelligence (Goleman),
56
"Emotional Intelligence" (Salovey
and Mayer), 5
emptiness, ego, 187
energy
excitement, 109–110
increased, ix–x
purpose, 180
redirecting, 70–73
Enron, employee comments, 188
enthusiasm, generating, 57
environment, imaginary, 92
errands, walking, 161
events, recognizing subtle, 173
examples
body work, 142–143
dealing with the loss of a company founder, 29–33

emotional discipline process,
25–29
emotional *Kung Fu*, 71–72
get a life, 202
inner jogging, 136
meditation, 90, 92
seeking happiness, 86–88
silence as a tool, 168–170
special moments, 174–176
therapeutic breathing, 125–126
excellence, fitness, 129
exercise
activity, 132
alternative forms, 148–151
breathing, 124–127
effect on body, 131
Pilates, 160
expectations
failed, 173–174
self-fulfillment, 112

failure
finding humor in, 139
vs. opportunity, 96–98
fear, study by the National
Institute of Health, 45–46
*Feeling Good: The New Mood
Therapy* (Burns), 61
feelings
acknowledgement, 42–43
experience, 10–11
feeling your, 63–67
life experience, 52
meaning, 49–54
moods, 51–53
old vs. new viewpoints, 53–54
rating physical, 27
suppression, 43
Feldman, Joel and Kate Feldman
(Conscious Relationship
Institute), Conscious
Dialogue, 189–190
Fengler, Fred and Todd Varnum,
Manifesting Your Heart's Desire,
113–115
1st level thinking, 106–107
Fisher, Roger and William Ury,
Getting to Yes, 70–72, 166

Salovey, P and J.D. Mayer,
    "Emotional Intelligence", 5
scars, removal, 115–116
Schweitzer, Albert, rekindling the
    inner spirit, 172–173
scripts, mental, 119
Seasonal Affective Disorder
    (SAD), 45
2nd level thinking, 107
self-deception, awareness, 43–44
self-image, improving, 116
self-talk, creative, 100–101
Seligman, Martin, *Learned
    Optimism*, 113
Selye, Hans, altruistic egoism, 181
sensitivity, subtle events, 172–174
September 11, reactions to, 64–65
service, opportunities for, 206
Shakespeare, William, changing
    roles, 99
Shaw, George Bernard, personal
    perspectives, 111
shiatsu, body work, 144
significance, finding, 202–203
silence, power of, 165–170
Somer, Elizabeth, *Food & Mood*,
    131
"Soul Song" (Manz), 203–204
spirit
    defined, 25
    focus beyond the self-centered
        ego, 207
    focusing on your, 28–29
    getting a life with, 201–205
    language of the, 15
    reactions, 24
    rekindling the inner, 172–173
Spontaneous Healing (Weil),
    124–127
sports
    competitive, 148
    participation, 161
stairs, vs. elevators, 161
statements, internal, 27–28, 31
steps, emotional discipline,
    23–25, 211
storms
    emotional, 75–80

internal, 76–77
strategies
    annoying situations, 101
    developing your own, 210–212
    difficult experiences, 102–103
    key decisions, 12
    mental imagery, 101–102
    self-talk, 100–101
    team, 37
stress
    massage therapy, 142–144
    Tai Chi, 149
studies, fear response, 45–46
submission, power, 40
subtlety, drama of, 171–177
suffering, avoiding, 63
suppression, feelings, 43
survivors, of concentration
    camps, 51–53
swings, mood, 76–77
syndrome, Asperger's, 45

Tai Chi, body work, 147–151
Tao Te Ching (Tzu), 70
techniques
    breathing, 124–127
    communication-mirroring,
        189–190
    FROM (arrow here) TO, 118
    Let Go and Let God, 192–193
    visualization, 118–119
thankfulness, being alive, 203
"The Eagle in the Sparrow"
    (Manz), 77–79
*The Heart of the Soul: Emotional
    Awareness* (Zukav and
    Francis), 61
The Medical Advisor (Time-Life
    Books)
    body work, 141
    breathing exercises, 124
*The Mozart Effect: Tapping the
    Power of Music to Heal the
    Body, Strengthen the Mind, and
    Unlock the Creative Spirit*
    (Campbell), 137
The New Psycho-Cybernetics
    (Maltz & Kennedy), 115–116

About the Author

~ ~ ~ ~ ~

Charles C. Manz, Ph.D., has been a student of emotional discipline his entire adult life. Most of his professional work over the past 20 years has specifically involved discovering and studying choices that we can make on a daily basis to become more effective while uplifting our life and spirit. He has applied all of the emotional discipline strategies offered in this book in his own life and continues to search for new creative ways to increase their benefits.

Dr. Manz is a speaker, consultant, and best-selling business author. He holds the Charles and Janet Nirenberg Chair of Business Leadership in the Isenberg School of Management at the University of Massachusetts. His work has been featured on radio and television and in *The Wall Street Journal, Fortune, U.S. News & World Report, Success,* and several other national publications. He received the prestigious Marvin Bower Fellowship at the Harvard Business School which is "awarded for outstanding achievement in research and productivity, influence, and leadership in business scholarship." He earned a Ph.D. in Business, with an emphasis in Organizational Behavior and Psychology, from The Pennsylvania State University and M.B.A. and B.A. degrees from Michigan State University.

He is the author or co-author of more than one hundred articles and 12 books, including the best-sellers *Business Without Bosses: How Self-Managing Teams Are Building High-Performing Companies*, the Stybel-Peabody prize winning *SuperLeadership: Leading Others to Lead Themselves*, *The Leadership Wisdom of Jesus: Practical Lessons For Today*, and *The New SuperLeadership: Leading Others to Lead Themselves*. His other books include *The Power of Failure: 27 Ways to Turn Life's Setbacks Into Success*, *The Wisdom of Solomon at Work: Ancient Virtues for Living and Leading Today*, *Mastering Self-Leadership: Empowering Yourself for Personal Excellence*, *Company of Heroes: Unleashing the Power of Self-Leadership*, *For Team Members Only: Making Your Workplace Team Productive and Hassle-Free*, *Team Work and Group Dynamics*, and *The Art of Self-Leadership: Strategies for Personal Effectiveness in Your Life and Work*. His books have been translated into many languages, and featured in book clubs and on audiotape.

Dr. Manz has served as a consultant for many organizations, including 3M, Ford, Motorola, Xerox, the Mayo Clinic, Procter & Gamble, General Motors, American Express, Allied Signal, Unisys, Josten's Learning, Banc One, the American Hospital Association, the American College of Physician Executives, and the U.S. and Canadian governments.

Berrett-Koehler Publishers

B errett-Koehler is an independent publisher of books
and other publications at the leading edge of new
thinking and innovative practice on work, business,
management, leadership, stewardship, career development, human resources, entrepreneurship, and global
sustainability.

Since the company's founding in 1992, we have been
committed to creating a world that works for all by
publishing books that help us to integrate our values
with our work and work lives, and to create more
humane and effective organizations.

We have chosen to focus on the areas of work,
business, and organizations, because these are central
elements in many people's lives today. Furthermore,
the work world is going through tumultuous changes,
from the decline of job security to the rise of new
structures for organizing people and work. We believe
that change is needed at all levels—individual, organizational, community, and global—and our publications
address each of these levels.

To find out about our new books,
special offers,
free excerpts,
and much more,
subscribe to our free monthly eNewsletter at

www.bkconnection.com

Please see next pages for other books
from Berrett-Koehler Publishers

The Leadership Wisdom of Jesus
Practical Lessons for Today

Charles Manz elucidates the spiritual and practical wisdom of Jesus' teachings. Remarkably contemporary, the lessons he presents point to a fresh approach that can enable both leaders and followers to maintain their integrity, live on a higher plane, and, ultimately, reach their personal and professional goals.

Paperback, 188 pages • ISBN 1-57675-066-3
Item #50663-415 $14.95

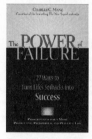

The Power of Failure
27 Ways to Turn Life's Setbacks into Success

Manz shows that failure is an essential component of personal and professional success. Using real-life examples and stories, this book offers inspiration and insight on how failure can provide us with the foundation for long-term success. Practical strategies show how these principles can be put to use immediately to fulfill your dreams.

Paperback • ISBN 1-57675-132-5 • Item #51325-415 $14.95

The Wisdom of Solomon at Work
Ancient Virtues for Living and Leading Today

Charles C. Manz, Karen P. Manz, Robert D. Marx, and Christopher P. Neck

The authors examine timeless questions of the human condition that have existed since ancient biblical times. Real-life stories—like that of Aaron Feuerstein who risked his life savings to breath life back into his company, Malden Mills, after a devastating fire—show how spiritual wisdom can intersect with work life.

Hardcover,150 pages • ISBN 1-57675-085-X
Item #5085X-415 $20.00

Berrett-Koehler Publishers
PO Box 565, Williston, VT 05495-9900
Call toll-free! **800-929-2929** 7 am-9 pm Eastern Standard Time
Or fax your order to 802-864-7627
For fastest service order online: **www.bkconnection.com**

Repacking Your Bags
Lighten Your Load for the Rest of Your Life, 2nd Edition

Richard J. Leider and David A. Shapiro

Learn how to climb out from under the many burdens you're carrying and find the fulfillment that's missing in your life. A simple yet elegant process teaches you to balance the demands of work, love, and place in order to create and live your own vision of success.

Paperback, 260 pages • ISBN 1-57675-180-5 • Item #51805-415 $16.95

The Power of Purpose
Creating Meaning in Your Life and Work

Richard J. Leider

We all possess a unique ability to do the work we were made for. Concise and easy to read, and including numerous stories of people living on purpose, *The Power of Purpose* is a remarkable tool to help you find your calling, an original guide to discovering the work you love to do.

Hardcover, 170 pages • ISBN 1-57675-021-3 • Item #50213-415 $20.00

Audiotape, 2 cassettes, 3 hours • ISBN 1-57453-215-4
Item #32154-415 $17.95

Beyond Juggling
Rebalancing Your Busy Life

Kurt Sandholtz, Brooklyn Derr, Kathy Buckner, and Dawn Carlson

Debunking the myth that juggling can ever lead to true balance, this book presents four alternative strategies for those who want to make both a living and a life— Alternating, Techflexing, Outsourcing, and Bundling— and helps readers choose those best suited to their needs. The authors explain each of the four strategies and include case studies of people who have used each method successfully to rebalance their lives.

Paperback, 240 pages • ISBN 1-57675-130-9 • Item #51309-415 $16.95

Hardcover • ISBN 1-57675-202-X Item #5202X-415 $24.95

Berrett-Koehler Publishers
PO Box 565, Williston, VT 05495-9900
Call toll-free! **800-929-2929** 7 am-9 pm Eastern Standard Time
Or fax your order to 802-864-7627
For fastest service order online: **www.bkconnection.com**

Berrett-Koehler books and audios are available at quantity discounts for orders of 10 or more copies.

Emotional Discipline
The Power to Choose How You Feel
Charles C. Manz

Paperback original
ISBN 1-57675 -230-5
Item #52305-415 $15.95

To find out about discounts on orders of 10 or more copies for individuals, corporations, institutions, and organizations, please call us toll-free at (800) 929-2929.

To find out about our discount programs for resellers, please contact our Special Sales department at (415) 288-0260; Fax: (415) 362-2512.

Or email us at bkpub@bkpub.com.

Berrett-Koehler Publishers
PO Box 565, Williston, VT 05495-9900
Call toll-free! **800-929-2929** 7 am-9 pm Eastern Standard Time
Or fax your order to 802-864-7627
For fastest service order online: **www.bkconnection.com**